The Cato Institute

The Cato Institute is named for the libertarian pamphlets *Cato's Letters,* which were inspired by the Roman Stoic Cato the Younger. Written by John Trenchard and Thomas Gordon, *Cato's Letters* were widely read in the American colonies in the early eighteenth century and played a major role in laying the philosophical foundation for the revolution that followed.

The erosion of civil and economic liberties in the modern world has occurred in concert with a widening array of social problems. These disturbing developments have resulted from a major failure to examine social problems in terms of the fundamental principles of human dignity, economic welfare, and justice.

The Cato Institute aims to broaden public policy debate by sponsoring programs designed to assist both the scholar and the concerned layperson in analyzing questions of political economy.

The programs of the Cato Institute include the sponsorship and publication of basic research in social philosophy and public policy; publication of major journals on the scholarship of liberty and commentary on political affairs; production of debate forums for radio; and organization of an extensive program of symposia, seminars, and conferences.

CATO INSTITUTE
747 Front Street
San Francisco, California 94111

Individualism
and the
Philosophy
of the
Social Sciences

Individualism
and the
Philosophy
of the
Social Sciences

Murray N. Rothbard

With a Foreword by Friedrich A. Hayek

CATO PAPER No. 4

INSTITUTE
San Francisco, California

ISBN: 0-932790-03-8

Printed in the United States of America.

CATO INSTITUTE
747 Front Street
San Francisco, California 94111

CONTENTS

FOREWORD

All in all, I am not fully convinced that the great flood of discussion on problems of scientific method that has appeared during the last few decades—albeit of high quality—has led to a great improvement in the scientific work that is forthcoming. I have myself been an avid reader of this literature, and it has undoubtedly taught me to avoid many mistakes. It has made me very much aware that the task of constructing helpful theories is much more difficult than I once imagined and that there are many pitfalls difficult to avoid. But unfortunately, much of it also suggests that there is a simple and easily learned procedure which one only has to follow carefully to arrive at valuable results. Of this I am becoming less and less convinced. The real difficulty still seems to be that of clearly stating the problem to which one wishes to find an answer. And on this, I fear, all my study of works on scientific method has hardly helped me. Yet it seems to encourage large numbers of young, and not so young, adepts of my discipline to treat the prescriptions of scientific method as if they were cookbook recipes which, if strictly followed, are certain to produce a nourishing dish.

Yet different problems require a very different procedure. If great advances have been made in some disciplines through the use of certain methods, this is no reason to expect that the same methods will be equally successful in other fields. In fact, the problems of such complex phenomena as we encounter in the biological or social sciences probably require a very different approach from that which has been so successful in the physical sciences. Among the thinkers who have made outstanding contributions to the peculiar problems raised by the science of human action, Ludwig von Mises has probably been the most acute and the most original in modern times. Professor Murray N. Rothbard has been profoundly influenced by his work in this field.

Both of us have been trying to develop it further, and if this has sometimes led us to modify Mises's conclusions, perhaps even in different directions, I am sure this is what Mises would have expected and even desired. The fruitfulness of a scholar's approach shows itself in the further developments to which it gives rise, and only further evolution can show which elaboration will in turn prove more fertile.

But minor differences, even if it is they which make every individual contribution worthwhile, are not what I wish to stress here. Professor Rothbard's writings are undoubtedly most helpful contributions to a great tradition. That the present state of this tradition, established by the large, systematic treatises that Mises completed from the third to the seventh decade of this century, should be made accessible to the readers of the ninth in a condensed form by one of his best-authorized disciples is certainly to be much welcomed. The issues examined have undoubtedly lost nothing of their importance. Every educated person will in the coming years have to learn to understand what praxeology is and what its particular methods are. In Mises's time it was certainly necessary to explain and justify its character in a critical examination of all the alternative approaches. But as the awareness of this new view spreads, simple and brief expositions of its essentials will be much needed. Professor Rothbard shows great skill in expounding them concisely in a language more familiar to the present generation.

In spite of what I said in the opening paragraph, methodology is important for the warning beacons it sets up against many of the intellectual fashions that still profoundlly influence political thought. And for those who do not themselves wish to enter philosophical controversy, the essays by Professor Rothbard reprinted here provide a most helpful guide to the understanding of those disputes on policy in which every thinking person must be interested. The essays are, of course, inevitably still of a certain intellectual difficulty, as anything of their quality must be. But at least those who are willing to make an effort should be able to derive much insight from their study and ought to be grateful to Professor Rothbard for providing so much in so short a space.

June 1979   F. A. Hayek

PART I:
The Mantle of Science

1. Introduction

In our proper condemnation of scientism in the study of man, we should not make the mistake of dismissing *science* as well. For if we do, we credit scientism too highly and accept at face value its claim to be the one and only scientific method. If scientism is, as we believe it to be, an improper method, then it cannot be truly scientific. Science, after all, means *scientia*, correct knowledge; it is older and wiser than the positivist-pragmatist attempt to monopolize the term.

Scientism is the profoundly unscientific attempt to transfer uncritically the methodology of the physical sciences to the study of human action. Both fields of inquiry must, it is true, be studied by the use of reason—the mind's identification of reality. But then it becomes crucially important, in reason, not to neglect the critical attribute of human action: that, alone in nature, human beings possess a rational consciousness. Stones, molecules, planets cannot *choose* their courses; their behavior is strictly and mechanically determined for them. Only human beings possess free will and consciousness: for they are conscious, and they can, and indeed must, choose their course of action.[1] To ignore this primordial fact about the nature of man—to ignore his volition, his free will—is to misconstrue the facts of reality and therefore to be profoundly and radically unscientific.

Man's necessity to choose means that, at any given time, he is acting to bring about some *end* in the immediate or distant future, i.e., that he has purposes. The steps that he takes to achieve his ends are his *means*. Man is born with no innate knowledge of what ends to choose or how to use which means to attain them.

---

[1] Human action, therefore, does not occur apart from cause; human beings *must* choose at any given moment, although the contents of the choice are *self-determined*.

3

Having no inborn knowledge of how to survive and prosper, he must learn what ends and means to adopt, and he is liable to make errors along the way. But only his reasoning mind can show him his goals and how to attain them.

We have already begun to build the first blocks of the many-storied edifice of the true sciences of man—and they are all grounded on the fact of man's volition.[2] On the formal fact that man uses means to attain ends, we ground the science of *praxeology*, or economics; *psychology* is the study of how and why man chooses the contents of his ends; *technology* tells what concrete means will lead to various ends; and *ethics* employs all the data of the various sciences to guide man toward the ends he should seek to attain, and therefore, by imputation, toward his proper means. None of these disciplines can make any sense whatever on scientistic premises. If men are like stones, if they are not purposive beings and do not strive for ends, then there is no economics, no psychology, no ethics, no technology, no science of man whatever.

---

[2]The sciences which deal with the functioning of man's automatic organs—physiology, anatomy, etc.—may be included in the physical sciences, for they are not based on man's will—although even here, psychosomatic medicine traces definite causal relations stemming from man's choices.

2. The Problem of Free Will

Before proceeding further, we must pause to consider the validity of free will, for it is curious that the determinist dogma has so often been accepted as the uniquely scientific position. And while many philosophers have demonstrated the existence of free will, the concept has all too rarely been applied to the "social sciences."

In the first place, each human being knows universally from introspection that he chooses. The positivists and behaviorists may scoff at introspection all they wish, but it remains true that the introspective knowledge of a conscious man that he is conscious and acts is a fact of reality. What, indeed, do the determinists have to offer to set against introspective fact? Only a poor and misleading analogy from the physical sciences. It is true that all mindless matter is determined and purposeless. But it is highly inappropriate, and moreover question-begging, simply and uncritically to apply the model of physics to man.

Why, indeed, should we accept determinism in nature? The reason we say that things are determined is that every existing thing must have a *specific* existence. Having a *specific* existence, it must have certain definite, definable, delimitable attributes, i.e., every thing must have a specific *nature*. Every being, then, can act or behave only in accordance with its nature, and any two beings can interact only in accord with their respective natures. Therefore, the actions of every being are caused by, determined by, its nature.[3]

---

[3] *See* Andrew G. Van Melsen, *The Philosophy of Nature* (Pittsburgh: Duquesne University Press, 1953), pp. 208 ff., 235 ff. While free will must be upheld for man, determinism must be equally upheld for physical nature. For a critique of the recent fallacious notion, based on the Heisenberg Uncertainty Principle, that atomic or subatomic particles have "free will," *see* Ludwig von Mises, *Theory and History* (New Haven: Yale University Press, 1957), pp. 87-92; and Albert H. Hobbs, *Social Problems and Scientism* (Harrisburg, Pa.: Stackpole, 1953), pp. 220-232.

But while most things have no consciousness and therefore pursue no goals, it is an essential attribute of *man's* nature that he has consciousness, and therefore that his actions are self-determined by the choices his mind makes.

At very best, the application of determinism to man is just an agenda for the future. After several centuries of arrogant proclamations, no determinist has come up with anything like a theory determining all of men's actions. Surely the burden of proof must rest on the one advancing a theory, particularly when the theory contradicts man's primary impressions. Surely we can, at the very least, tell the determinists to keep quiet until they can offer their determinations—including, of course, their advance determinations of each of our reactions to their determining theory. But there is far more that can be said. For determinism, as applied to man, is a self-contradictory thesis, since the man who employs it relies implicitly on the existence of free will. If we are determined in the ideas we accept, then X, the determinist, is determined to believe in determinism, while Y, the believer in free will, is also determined to believe in his own doctrine. Since man's mind is, according to determinism, not free to think and come to conclusions about reality, it is absurd for X to try to convince Y or anyone else of the truth of determinism. In short, the determinist must rely, for the spread of his ideas, on the nondetermined, free-will choices of others, on their free will to adopt or reject ideas.[4] In the same way, the various brands of determinists—behaviorists, positivists, Marxists, etc.—implicitly claim special exemption for themselves from their own determined systems.[5] But if a man cannot affirm a proposition without employing its negation, he is not only caught in an inextricable self-contradiction; *he is con-*

---

[4]"Even the controversial writings of the mechanists themselves appear to be intended for readers endowed with powers of choice. In other words, the determinist who would win others to his way of thinking must write as if he himself, and his readers at least, had freedom of choice, while all the rest of mankind are mechanistically determined in thought and in conduct." Francis L. Harmon, *Principles of Psychology* (Milwaukeee: Bruce, 1938), p. 497 and pp.493-499. *See also* Joseph D. Hassett, S. J., Robert A. Mitchell, S. J., and J. Donald Monan, S. J., *The Philosophy of Human Knowing* (Westminster, Md.: Newman Press, 1953), pp. 71-72.

[5]*See* Mises, *Theory and History,* pp. 258-260, and Mises, *Human Action* (New Haven: Yale University Press, 1949), pp. 74 ff.

ceding to the negation the status of an axiom.[6]

A corollary self-contradiction: The determinists profess to be able, some day, to determine what man's choices and actions will be. But, on their own grounds, their own knowledge of this determining theory is itself determined. How then can they aspire to know *all*, if the extent of their *own* knowledge is itself determined, and therefore arbitrarily delimited? In fact, if our ideas are determined, then we have no way of freely revising our judgments and of learning truth—whether the truth of determinism or of anything else.[7]

Thus, the determinist, to advocate his doctrine, must place himself and his theory outside the allegedly universally determined realm, i.e., he must employ free will. This reliance of determinism on its negation is an instance of a wider truth: that it is self-contradictory to use reason in any attempt to deny the validity of reason as a means of attaining knowledge. Such self-contradiction is implicit in such currently fashionable sentiments as "reason shows us that reason is weak," or "the more we know, the more we know how little we know."[8]

Some may object that man is not really free because he must obey natural laws. To say that man is not free because he is not

---

[6] Phillips therefore calls this attribute of an axiom a "boomerang principle . . . for even though we cast it away from us, it returns to us again," and illustrates by showing that an attempt to deny the Aristotelian law of noncontradiction must end by assuming it. R. P. Phillips, *Modern Thomistic Philosophy,* 2 vols. (Westminster, Md.: Newman Bookshop, 1934-35), 2:36-37. *See also* John J. Toohey, S. J., *Notes on Epistemology* (Washington, D.C.: Georgetown University, 1952), passim, and Murray N. Rothbard, "In Defense of 'Extreme Apriorism,'" *Southern Economic Journal,* January 1957, p. 318.

[7] In the course of a critique of determinism, Phillips wrote: "What purpose . . . could advice serve if we were unable to revise a judgment we had formed, and so act in a different way to which we at first intended?" Phillips, *Modern Thomistic Philosophy,* 1:282.

For stress on free will as freedom to think, to employ reason, *see* Robert L. Humphrey, "Human Nature in American Thought," *Political Science Quarterly,* June 1954, p. 269; J. F. Leibell, ed., *Readings in Ethics* (Chicago: Loyola University Press, 1926), pp. 90, 103, 109; Robert Edward Brennan, O.P., *Thomistic Psychology* (New York: Macmillan, 1941), pp. 221-222; Van Melsen, *Philosophy of Nature,* pp. 235-236; and Mises, *Theory and History,* pp. 177-179.

[8] "A man involves himself in a contradiction when he uses the reasoning of the intellect to prove that that reasoning cannot be relied upon." Toohey, *Notes on Epistemology,* p. 29. *See also* Phillips, *Modern Thomistic Philosophy,* 2:16, and Frank Thilly, *A History of Philosophy* (New York: Henry Holt, 1914), p. 586.

able to do anything he may possibly desire, however, confuses freedom and power.[9] It is clearly absurd to employ as a definition of "freedom" the power of an entity to perform an impossible action, to violate its nature.[10]

Determinists often imply that a man's ideas are necessarily determined by the ideas of others, of "society." Yet A and B can hear the same idea propounded; A can adopt it as valid while B will not. Each man, therefore, has the free choice of adopting or not adopting an idea or value. It is true that many men may uncritically adopt the ideas of others; yet this process cannot regress infinitely. At some point in time, the idea originated, i.e., the idea was *not* taken from others but was arrived at by some mind independently and creatively. This is logically necessary for any given idea. "Society," therefore, cannot dictate ideas. If someone grows up in a world where people generally believe that "all redheads are demons," he is free, as he grows up, to rethink the problem and arrive at a different conclusion. If this were not true, ideas, once adopted, could never have been changed.

We conclude, therefore, that true science decrees determinism for physical nature and free will for man, and for the same reason: that every thing must act in accordance with its specific nature. And since men are free to adopt ideas and to act upon them, it is never events or stimuli external to the mind that *cause* its ideas; rather the mind freely adopts ideas about external events. A savage, an infant, and a civilized man will react in entirely different ways to the sight of the same stimulus—be it a fountain pen, an alarm clock, or a machine gun, for each mind has different ideas about the object's meaning and qualities.[11] Let us therefore never again say that the Great Depression of the 1930s *caused* men to adopt socialism or interventionism (or that poverty *causes* people to adopt Communism). The depression existed, and men were moved to think about this striking event; but that they adopted

[9] *See* F. A. Hayek, *The Road to Serfdom* (Chicago: University of Chicago Press, 1944), p. 26.

[10] John G. Vance, "Freedom," quoted in Leibell, ed., *Readings in Ethics,* pp. 98-100. *See also* Van Melsen, *Philosophy of Nature,* p. 236, and Michael Maher, *Psychology,* quoted in Leibell, p. 90.

[11] Thus, cf. C. I. Lewis, *Mind and the World Order* (New York: Dover Publications, 1956), pp. 49-51.

socialism or its equivalent as the way out was not determined by the event; they might just as well have chosen laissez-faire or Buddhism or any other attempted solution. The deciding factor was the *idea* that people chose to adopt.

What *led* the people to adopt particular ideas? Here the historian may enumerate and weigh various factors, but he must always stop short at the ultimate freedom of the will. Thus, in any given matter, a person may freely decide either to think about a problem independently or to accept uncritically the ideas offered by others. Certainly, most of the people, especially in abstract matters, choose to follow the ideas offered by the intellectuals. At the time of the Great Depression, there were a host of intellectuals offering the nostrum of statism or socialism as a cure for the depression, while very few suggested laissez-faire or absolute monarchy.

The realization that ideas, freely adopted, determine social institutions, and not vice versa, illuminates many critical areas of the study of man. Rousseau and his host of modern followers, who hold that man is good but is corrupted by his institutions, must finally wither under the query: And who but *men* created these institutions? The tendency of many modern intellectuals to worship the primitive (also the childlike—especially the child "progressively" educated—the "natural" life of the noble savage of the South Seas, etc.) has perhaps the same roots. We are also told repeatedly that differences between largely isolated tribes and ethnic groups are "culturally determined": tribe X being intelligent or peaceful because of its X-culture; tribe Y, dull or warlike because of Y-culture. If we fully realize that the men of each tribe created its own culture (unless we are to assume its creation by some mystic *deus ex machina*), we see that this popular "explanation" is no better than explaining the sleep-inducing properties of opium by its "dormitive power." Indeed, it is worse, because it adds the error of social determinism.

It will undoubtedly be charged that this discussion of free will and determinism is "one-sided" and that it leaves out the alleged fact that all of life is multicausal and interdependent. We must not forget, however, that the very goal of science is simpler explanations of wider phenomena. In this case, we are confronted

9

with the fact that there can logically be only one *ultimate sovereign* over a man's actions: either his own free will or some cause outside that will. There is no other alternative, there is no middle ground, and therefore the fashionable eclecticism of modern scholarship must in this case yield to the hard realities of the Law of the Excluded Middle.

If free will has been vindicated, how can we prove the existence of consciousness itself? The answer is simple: to *prove* means to make evident something not yet evident. Yet some propositions may be already evident to the self, i.e., self-evident. A self-evident axiom, as we have indicated, will be a proposition that cannot be contradicted without employing the axiom itself in the attempt. And the existence of consciousness is not only evident to all of us through direct introspection, but is also a fundamental axiom, for the very act of doubting consciousness must itself be performed by a consciousness.[12] Thus, the behaviorist who spurns consciousness for "objective" laboratory data must rely on the consciousness of his laboratory associates to report the data to him.

The key to scientism is its denial of the existence of individual consciousness and will.[13] This takes two main forms: applying mechanical analogies from the physical sciences to individual men, and applying organismic analogies to such fictional collective wholes as "society." The latter course attributes consciousness and will, not to individuals, but to some collective organic whole of which the individual is merely a determined cell. Both methods are aspects of the rejection of individual consciousness.

[12] *See* Hassett, Mitchell, and Monan, *Philosophy of Human Knowing*, pp. 33-35. *See also* Phillips, *Modern Thomistic Philosophy*, 1:50-51; Toohey, *Notes on Epistemology*, pp. 5, 36, 101, 107-108; and Thilly, *History of Philosophy*, p. 363.
[13] Professor Strausz-Hupé also makes this point in his paper in this symposium.

3. The False Mechanical Analogies of Scientism

The scientific method in the study of man is almost wholly one of building on analogies from the physical sciences. Some of the common mechanistic analogies follow.

Man as Servomechanism: Just as Bertrand Russell, one of the leaders of scientism, reverses reality by attributing determinism to men and free will to physical particles, so it has recently become the fashion to say that modern machines "think," while man is merely a complex form of machine, or "servomechanism."[14] What is overlooked here is that machines, no matter how complex, are simply devices made by man to serve man's purposes and goals; their actions are preset by their creators, and the machines can never act in any other way or suddenly adopt new goals and act upon them. They cannot do so, finally, because the machines are not alive and are therefore certainly not conscious. If men are machines, on the other hand, then the determinists, in addition to meeting the above critique, must answer the question: Who created *men* and for what purpose?—a rather embarrassing question for materialists to answer.[15]

Social Engineering: This term implies that men are no different from stones or other physical objects, and therefore that they should be blueprinted and reshaped in the same way as objects by

---

[14] *See* Mises, *Theory and History,* p. 92.

[15] "A machine is a device made by man. It is the realization of a design and it runs precisely according to the plan of its authors. What produces the product of its operation is not something within it but the purpose the constructor wanted to realize by means of its construction. It is the constructor and operator who create and produce, not the machine. To ascribe to a machine any activity is anthropomorphism and animism. The machine . . . does not move; it is put into motion by men." Ibid., pp. 94-95.

"social" engineers. When Rex Tugwell wrote in his famous poem during the flush days of the New Deal:

> I have gathered my tools and my charts,
> My plans are finished and practical.
> I shall roll up my sleeves—make America over.

one wonders whether his admiring readers thought themselves to be among the directing engineers or among the raw material that would be "made over."[16]

Model-building: Economics and political science have been beset by a plague of "model-building."[17] People do not construct theories anymore; they "build" models of the society or economy. Yet no one seems to notice the peculiar inaptness of the concept. An engineering model is an exact replica in miniature, i.e., in exact quantitative proportion, of the relationships existing in the given structure in the real world; but the "models" of economic and political theory are simply a few equations and concepts which, at very best, could only approximate a few of the numerous relations in the economy or society.

Measurement: The Econometric Society's original motto was "Science is measurement," this ideal having been transferred intact from the natural sciences. The frantic and vain attempts to measure intensive psychic magnitudes in psychology and in economics would disappear if it were realized that the very concept of measurement implies the necessity for an objective *extensive* unit to serve as a measure. But the magnitudes in consciousness are necessarily *intensive* and therefore not capable of measurement.[18]

---

[16] Ibid., pp. 249-250.

[17] On this and many other points in this paper I am greatly indebted to Ludwig von Mises and to his development of the science of praxeology. *See* Ludwig von Mises, "Comment about the Mathematical Treatment of Economic Problems," *Studium Generale,* vol. 6 (1953), no. 2; Mises, *Human Action,* passim; and Mises, *Theory and History,* pp. 240-263. The foundations of praxeology as a method were laid by the English classical economist Nassau Senior. Unfortunately, the positivistic John Stuart Mill's side of their methodological debate became much better known than Senior's. *See* Marian Bowley, *Nassau Senior and Classical Economics* (New York: Kelley, 1949), chap. 1, especially pp. 64-65.

[18] For a critique of recent attempts to fashion a new theory of measurement for intensive magnitudes, *see* Murray N. Rothbard, "Toward a Reconstruction of Utility and Welfare Economics," in *On Freedom and Free Enterprise: Essays in Honor of Ludwig von Mises,* ed. M. Sennholz (Princeton: Van Nostrand, 1956), pp. 241-243.

The Mathematical Method: Not only measurement, but the use of mathematics in general, in the social sciences and philosophy today is an illegitimate transfer from physics. In the first place, a mathematical equation implies the existence of quantities that can be equated, which in turn implies a unit of measurement for these quantities. Secondly, mathematical relations are *functional;* i.e., variables are interdependent, and identifying the causal variable depends on which is held as given and which is changed. This methodology is appropriate in physics, where entities do not themselves provide the causes for their actions but are instead determined by discoverable quantitative laws of their nature and the nature of the interacting entities. But in human action, the free-will choice of the human consciousness is the cause, and this cause generates certain effects. The mathematical concept of interdetermining "function" is therefore inappropriate.

Indeed, the very concept of "variable" used so frequently in econometrics is illegitimate, for physics is able to arrive at laws only by discovering *constants.* The concept of "variable" only makes sense if there are some things that are *not* variable, but constant. Yet in human action, free will precludes any quantitative constants (including constant units of measurement). All attempts to discover such constants (such as the strict quantity theory of money or the Keynesian "consumption function") were inherently doomed to failure.

Finally, such staples of mathematical economics as the calculus are completely inappropriate for human action because they assume infinitely small continuity; while such concepts may legitimately describe the completely determined path of a physical particle, they are seriously misleading in describing the willed action of a human being. Such willed action can occur only in discrete, non-infinitely-small steps, steps large enough to be perceivable by a human consciousness. Hence the continuity assumptions of calculus are inappropriate for the study of man.

Other metaphors bodily and misleadingly transplanted from physics include *equilibrium, elasticity, statics and dynamics, velocity of circulation,* and *friction.* Equilibrium in physics is a state in which an entity remains; but in economics or politics there is never really such an equilibrium state existing; there is but a

13

tendency in that direction. Moreover, the term *equilibrium* has emotional connotations, and so it was only a brief step to the further mischief of holding up equilibrium as not only possible, but as the ideal by which to gauge all existing institutions. But since man, by his very nature, must keep acting, he cannot be in equilibrium while he lives, and therefore the ideal, being impossible, is also inappropriate.

The concept of *friction* is used in a similar way. Some economists, for example, have assumed that men have "perfect knowledge," that the factors of production have "perfect mobility," etc., and then have airily dismissed all difficulties in applying these absurdities to the real world as simple problems of "friction," just as the physical sciences bring in friction to add to their "perfect" framework. These assumptions in fact make *omniscience* the standard or ideal, and this cannot exist by the nature of man.

4. The False Organismic Analogies of Scientism

The organismic analogies attribute consciousness, or other organic qualities, to "social wholes" which are really only labels for the interrelations of individuals.[19] Just as in the mechanistic metaphors individual men are subsumed and determined, here they become mindless cells in some sort of social organism. While few people today would assert flatly that "society is an organism," most social theorists hold doctrines that imply this. Note, for example, such phrases as "society determines the values of its individual members," or "the culture determines the actions of individual members," or "the individual's actions are determined by the role he plays in the group to which he belongs," etc. Such concepts as "the public good," "the common good," "social welfare," etc., are also endemic. All these concepts rest on the implicit premise that there exists, somewhere, a living organic entity known as "society," "the group," "the public," "the community," and that that entity has values and pursues ends.

Not only are these terms held up as living entities; they are supposed to exist *more* fundamentally than do mere individuals, and certainly "their" goals take precedence over individual ones. It is ironic that the self-proclaimed apostles of "science" should pursue the sheer mysticism of assuming the living reality of these concepts.[20] Such concepts as "public good," "general welfare," etc., should, therefore, be discarded as grossly unscientific, and

---

[19]On the fallacy of conceptual realism (or Platonic ultrarealism) involved here, and on the necessity for methodological individualism, *see* F. A. Hayek, *The Counter-Revolution of Science* (Glencoe, Ill.: Free Press, 1955), passim, and Mises, *Human Action*, pp. 41 ff. and 45 ff.

[20]We may therefore say with Frank Chodorov that "society are people." Frank Chodorov, "Society Are People," in *The Rise and Fall of Society* (New York: Devin-Adair, 1959), pp. 29-37. For a critique of the mystique of "society," *see* Mises, *Theory and History*, p. 250 ff.

the next time someone preaches the priority of "public good" over the individual good, we must ask: Who *is* the "public" in this case? We must remember that in the slogan justifying the public debt that rose to fame in the 1930s, "We owe it only to ourselves," it makes a big difference for every man whether he is a member of the "we" or of the "ourselves."[21]

A similar fallacy is committed, both by friends and foes of the market economy, when the market is called "impersonal." Thus, people often complain that the market is too "impersonal" because it does not grant to them a greater share of worldly goods. It is overlooked that the "market" is not some sort of living entity making good or bad decisions, but is simply a label for individual persons and their voluntary interactions. If A thinks that the "impersonal market" is not paying him enough, he is *really* saying that individuals B, C, and D are not willing to pay him as much as he would like to receive. The "market" is individuals acting. Similarly, if B thinks that the "market" is not paying A enough, B is perfectly free to step in and supply the difference. He is not blocked in this effort by some monster named "market."

One example of the widespread use of the organismic fallacy is in discussions of international trade. Thus, during the gold-standard era, how often did the cry go up that "England" or "France" or some other country was in mortal danger because "it" was "losing gold"? What was actually happening was that English*men* or French*men* were voluntarily shipping gold overseas and thus threatening the banks in those countries with the necessity of meeting obligations (to pay in gold) which they could not possibly fulfill. But the use of the organismic metaphor converted a grave problem of banking into a vague national crisis for which every citizen was somehow responsible.[22]

So far we have been discussing those organismic concepts which assume the existence of a fictive consciousness in some collective

[21] *See* the delightful essay by Frank Chodorov, "We Lose It to Ourselves," *Analysis,* June 1950, p. 3.

[22] A similar error of metaphor prevails in foreign policy matters. Thus: "When one uses the simple monosyllabic 'France,' one thinks of France as a unit, an entity. When . . . we say 'France sent *her* troops to conquer Tunis'—we impute not only unity but personality to the country. The very words conceal the facts and make international relations a glamorous drama in which personalized nations are the

whole. There are also numerous examples of other misleading biological analogies in the study of man. We hear much, for example, of "young" and "old" nations, as if an American aged twenty is somehow "younger" than a Frenchman of the same age. We read of "mature economies," as if an economy must grow rapidly and then become "mature." The current fashion of an "economics of growth" presumes that every economy is somehow destined, like a living organism, to "grow" in some predetermined manner at a definite rate. (In the enthusiasm it is overlooked that too many economies "grow" backward.) That all of these analogies are attempts to negate individual will and consciousness has been pointed out by Edith Tilton Penrose. Referring to biological analogies as applied to business firms, she writes:

> . . . where explicit biological analogies crop up in economics they are drawn exclusively from that aspect of biology which deals with the nonmotivated behavior of organisms. . . . So it is with the life-cycle analogy. We have no reason whatever for thinking that the growth pattern of a biological organism is *willed* by the organism itself. On the other hand, we have every reason for thinking that the growth of a firm is willed by those who make the decisions of the firm . . . and the proof of this lies in the fact that no one can describe the development of any given firm . . . except in terms of decisions taken by individual men.[23]

---

actors, and all too easily we forget the flesh-and-blood men and women who are the true actors. . . . If we had no such word as 'France' . . . then we should more accurately describe the Tunis expedition in some such way as this: 'A few of . . . thirty-eight million persons sent thirty thousand others to conquer Tunis.' This way of putting the fact immediately suggests a question, or rather a series of questions. Who were the 'few'? Why did they send the thirty thousand to Tunis? And why did these obey? Empire-building is done not by 'nations,' but by men. The problem before us is to discover the men, the active, interested minorities in each nation, who are directly interested in imperialism and then to analyze the reasons why the majorities pay the expenses and fight the wars. . . ." Parker Thomas Moon, *Imperialism and World Politics* (New York: Macmillan, 1930), p. 58.
[23] Edith Tilton Penrose, "Biological Analogies in the Theory of the Firm," *American Economic Review,* December 1952, p. 808.

5. Axioms and Deductions

The fundamental axiom, then, for the study of man is the existence of individual consciousness, and we have seen the numerous ways in which scientism tries to reject or avoid this axiom. Not being omniscient, a man must learn; he must ever adopt ideas and act upon them, choosing ends and the means to attain these ends. Upon this simple fundamental axiom a vast deductive edifice can be constructed. Professor Ludwig von Mises has already done this for economics, which he has subsumed under the science of praxeology: This centers on the universal formal fact that all men use means for chosen ends, without investigating the processes of the concrete choices or the justification for them. Mises has shown that the entire structure of economic thought can be deduced from this axiom (with the help of a very few subsidiary axioms).[24]

Since the fundamental and other axioms are qualitative by nature, it follows that the propositions deduced by the laws of logic from these axioms are also qualitative. The laws of human action are therefore qualitative, and in fact it should be clear that free will precludes quantitative laws. Thus, we may set forth the absolute economic law that an increase in the supply of a good, given the demand, will lower its price; but if we attempted to prescribe with similar generality *how much* the price would fall,

[24]In Mises, *Human Action.* For a defense of this method, *see* Rothbard, "In Defense of 'Extreme Apriorism,'" *Southern Economic Journal,* January 1957, pp. 314-320; and Rothbard, "Praxeology: Reply to Mr. Schuller," *American Economic Review,* December 1951, pp. 943-946.

given a definite increase in supply, we would shatter against the free-will rock of varying valuations by different individuals.

It goes without saying that the axiomatic-deductive method has been in disrepute in recent decades, in all disciplines but mathematics and formal logic—and even here the axioms are often supposed to be a mere convention rather than necessary truth. Few discussions of the history of philosophy or scientific method fail to make the ritual attacks on old-fashioned argumentation from self-evident principles. And yet the disciples of scientism themselves implicitly assume as self-evident *not* what cannot be contradicted, but simply that the methodology of physics is the only truly scientific methodology. This methodology, briefly, is to look at facts, then frame ever more general hypotheses to account for the facts, and then to test these hypotheses by experimentally verifying other deductions made from them. But this method is appropriate only in the physical sciences, where we begin by knowing external sense data and then proceed to our task of trying to find, as closely as we can, the causal laws of behavior of the entities we perceive. We have no way of knowing these laws directly; but fortunately we may verify them by performing controlled laboratory experiments to test propositions deduced from them. In these experiments we can vary one factor, while keeping all other relevant factors constant. Yet the process of accumulating knowledge in physics is always rather tenuous; and, as has happened, as we become more and more abstract, there is greater possibility that some other explanation will be devised which fits more of the observed facts and which may then replace the older theory.

In the study of human action, on the other hand, the proper procedure is the reverse. Here we *begin* with the primary axioms; we know that men are the causal agents, that the ideas they adopt by free will govern their actions. We therefore begin by fully knowing the abstract axioms, and we may then build upon them by logical deduction, introducing a few subsidiary axioms to limit the range of the study to the concrete applications we care about. Furthermore, in human affairs, the existence of free will prevents us from conducting any controlled experiments; for people's ideas and valuations are continually subject to change, and therefore nothing can be held constant. The proper theoretical methodology in human affairs, then, is the axiomatic-deductive method. The laws deduced by this method are *more*, not less, firmly grounded than the laws of physics; for since the ultimate causes are known directly as true, their consequents are also true.

One of the reasons for the scientistic hatred of the axiomatic-deductive method is historical. Thus, Dr. E. C. Harwood, inveterate battler for the pragmatic method in economics and the social sciences, criticizes Mises as follows:

> Like the Greeks, Dr. Von Mises disparages change. "Praxeology is not concerned with the changing content of acting, but with its pure form and categorial structure." No one who appreciates the long struggle of man toward more adequate knowing would criticize Aristotle for his adoption of a similar viewpoint 2,000 years ago, but, after all, that *was* 2,000 years ago; surely economists can do better than seek light on their subject from a beacon that was extinguished by the Galilean revolution in the 17th century.[25]

Apart from the usual pragmatist antagonism to the apodictic laws of logic, this quotation embodies a typical historiographic myth. The germ of truth in the historical picture of the noble Galileo versus the antiscientific Church consists largely in two important errors of Aristotle: (a) he thought of physical entities as acting teleologically, and thus in a sense as being causal agents; and (b) he necessarily had no knowledge of the experimental method, which had not yet been developed, and therefore thought that the axiomatic-deductive-qualitative method was the only one appropriate to the *physical* as well as to the human sciences. When the seventeenth century enthroned quantitative laws and laboratory methods, the partially justified repudiation of Aristotle in physics was followed by the unfortunate expulsion of Aristotle

[25]E. C. Harwood, *Reconstruction of Economics* (Great Barrington, Mass.: American Institute for Economic Research, 1955), p. 39. On this and other examples of scientism, *see* Leland B. Yeager, "Measurement as Scientific Method in Economics," *American Journal of Economics and Sociology*, July 1957, p. 337. *See also* Yeager, "Reply to Col. Harwood," *American Journal of Economics and Sociology*, October 1957, pp. 104-106. As Yeager wisely concludes: "Anthropomorphism, rightly scorned in the natural sciences as prescientific metaphysics, is justified in economics because economics is about human action."

and his methodology from the human sciences as well.[26] This is true apart from historical findings that the Scholastics of the Middle Ages were the forerunners, rather than the obscurantist enemies, of experimental physical science.[27]

One example of concrete law deduced from our fundamental axiom is as follows: Since all action is determined by the choice of the actor, any particular act demonstrates a person's preference for this action. From this it follows that if A and B voluntarily agree to make an exchange (whether the exchange be material or spiritual), both parties are doing so because they expect to benefit.[28]

[26] See Van Melson, *Philosophy of Nature,* pp. 54-58, 1-16.

[27] As Schumpeter declared: "The scholastic science of the Middle Ages contained all the germs of the laical science of the Renaissance." The experimental method was used notably by Friar Roger Bacon and Peter of Maricourt in the thirteenth century; the heliocentric system of astronomy originated *inside* the Church (Cusanus was a cardinal and Copernicus a canonist); and the Benedictine monks led the way in developing medieval engineering. See Joseph A. Schumpeter, *History of Economic Analysis* (New York: Oxford University Press, 1954), p. 81 ff.; and Lynn White, Jr., "Dynamo and Virgin Reconsidered," *The American Scholar,* Spring 1958, pp. 183-212.

[28] For a refutation of the charge that this is a circular argument, *see* Rothbard, "Toward a Reconstruction of Utility and Welfare Economics," in Sennholz, ed., *On Freedom and Free Enterprise,* p. 228.

6. Science and Values: Arbitrary Ethics

Having discussed the properly scientific, as contrasted to the scientistic, approach to the study of man, we may conclude by briefly considering the age-old question of the relationship between science and values. Ever since Max Weber, the dominant position in the social sciences, at least *de jure*, has been *Wertfreiheit:* that science itself must not make value judgments, but confine itself to judgments of fact, since ultimate ends can be only sheer personal preference not subject to rational argument. The classical philosophical view that a rational (i.e., in the broad sense of the term, a "scientific") ethic is possible has been largely discarded. As a result, the critics of *Wertfreiheit*, having dismissed the possibility of rational ethics as a separate discipline, have taken to smuggling in arbitrary, *ad hoc* ethical judgments through the back door of each particular science of man. The current fashion is to preserve a facade of *Wertfreiheit*, while casually adopting value judgments, not as the scientist's own decision, but as the consensus of the values of others. Instead of choosing his own ends and valuing accordingly, the scientist supposedly maintains his neutrality by adopting the values of the bulk of society. In short, to set forth one's own values is now considered biased and "nonobjective," while to adopt uncritically the slogans of other people is the height of "objectivity." Scientific objectivity no longer means a man's pursuit of truth wherever it may lead, but abiding by a Gallup poll of other, less informed subjectivities.[29]

The attitude that value judgments are self-evidently correct because "the people" hold them permeates social science. The social scientist often claims that he is merely a technician, advising his

[29] "When they [the practical scientists] remember their vows of objectivity, they get other people to make their judgments for them." Anthony Standen, *Science Is a Sacred Cow* (New York: Dutton, 1958), p. 165.

clients—the public—how to attain their ends, whatever they may be. And he believes that he thereby can take a value position without really committing himself to any values of his own. Here is an example of this attitude, taken from a recent public-finance textbook (an area where the economic scientist must constantly confront ethical problems):

> The present-day justification for the ability principle (among economists) is simply the fact that . . . it is in accord with consensus of attitudes toward equity in the distribution of real income and of tax burden. Equity questions always involve value judgments, and tax structures can be evaluated, from an equity standpoint, only in terms of their relative conformity with the consensus of thought in the particular society with respect to equity.[30]

But the scientist cannot thereby escape making value judgments of his own. A man who knowingly advises a criminal gang on the best means of safe-cracking is thereby implicitly endorsing the end: safe-cracking. He is an accessory before the fact. An economist who advises the public on the most efficient method of obtaining economic equality is endorsing the end: economic equality. The economist who advises the Federal Reserve System how most expeditiously to manage the economy is thereby endorsing the existence of the system and its aim of stabilization. A political scientist who advises a government bureau on how to reorganize its staff for greater efficiency (or less inefficiency) is thereby endorsing the existence and the success of that bureau. To be convinced of this, consider what the proper course would be for an economist who *opposes* the existence of the Federal Reserve System, or the political scientist who would like to see the liquidation of the bureau. Wouldn't he be betraying his principles if he helped what he is against to become more efficient? Wouldn't his proper course either be to refuse to advise it, or perhaps to try to promote its *in*efficiency—on the grounds of the classic remark by a great American industrialist (speaking of government corruption): "Thank God that we don't get as much government as we pay for"?

It should be realized that values do not become true or legiti-

[30] John F. Due, *Government Finance* (Homewood, Ill.: Irwin, 1954), p. 122.

mate because many people hold them; and their popularity does not make them self-evident. Economics abounds in instances of arbitrary values smuggled into works the authors of which would never think of engaging in ethical analysis or propounding an ethical system. The virtue of equality, as we have indicated, is simply taken for granted without justification; and it is established, not by sense perception of reality or by showing that its negation is self-contradictory—the true criteria of self-evidence—but by assuming that anyone who disagrees is a knave and a rogue. Taxation is a realm where arbitrary values flourish, and we may illustrate by analyzing the most hallowed and surely the most commonsensical of all tax ethics: some of Adam Smith's famous canons of "justice" in taxation.[31] These canons have since been treated as self-evident gospel in practically every work on public finance. Take, for example, the canon that the costs of collection of any tax be kept to a minimum. Obvious enough to include in the most *wertfrei* treatise? Not at all—for we must not overlook the point of view of the *tax collectors*. They will favor high administrative costs of taxation, simply because high costs mean greater opportunities for bureaucratic employment. On what possible grounds can we call the bureaucrat "wrong" or "unjust"? Certainly no ethical system has been offered. Furthermore, if the tax itself is considered bad on other grounds, then the opponent of the tax may well favor high administrative costs on the grounds that there will then be less chance for the tax to do damage by being fully collected.

Consider another seemingly obvious Smith canon, viz., that a tax be levied so that payment is convenient. But again, this is by no means self-evident. Opponents of a tax, for example, may want the tax to be made purposely inconvenient so as to induce the people to rebel against the levy. Or another: that a tax be certain and not arbitrary, so that the taxpayers know what they will have to pay. But here again, further analysis raises many problems. For some may argue that uncertainty positively benefits the taxpayers, for it makes requirements more flexible, thus allowing

---

[31] Adam Smith, *The Wealth of Nations* (New York: Modern Library, 1937), pp. 777-779.

more room for possible bribery of the tax collector. Another popular maxim is that a tax be framed to make it difficult to evade. But again, if a tax is considered unjust, evasion might be highly beneficial, economically and morally.

The purpose of these strictures has not been to defend high costs of tax collection, inconvenient taxes, bribery, or evasion, but to show that even the tritest bits of ethical judgments in economics are completely illegitimate. And they are illegitimate whether one believes in *Wertfreiheit* or in the possibility of a rational ethic: for such *ad hoc* ethical judgments violate the canons of either school. They are neither *wertfrei* nor are they supported by any systematic analysis.

7. Conclusion

Surveying the attributes of the proper science of man as against scientism, one finds a shining, clear thread separating one from the other. The true science of man bases itself upon the *existence of individual human beings*, upon individual life and consciousness. The scientific brethren (dominant in modern times) range themselves always against the meaningful existence of individuals: The biologists deny the existence of life, the psychologists deny consciousness, the economists deny economics, and the political theorists deny political philosophy. What they *affirm* is the existence and primacy of social wholes: "society," the "collective," the "group," the "nation." The individual, they assert, must be value-free himself, but must take his values from "society." The true science of man concentrates on the individual as of central, epistemological, and ethical importance; the adherents of scientism, in contrast, lose no opportunity to denigrate the individual and submerge him in the importance of the collective. With such radically contrasting epistemologies, it is hardly sheer coincidence that the political views of the two opposing camps tend to be individualist and collectivist, respectively.

PART II:
Praxeology as the Method of the Social Sciences

1. The Praxeological Method

During the past generation, a veritable revolution has taken place in the discipline of economics. I am referring not so much to the well-known Keynesian revolution, but to the quieter yet more profound revolution in the methodology of the discipline. This change has not occurred simply in the formal writings of the handful of conscious methodologists; it has spread, largely unnoticed, until it now permeates research and study in all parts of the field. Some effects of this methodological revolution are all too apparent. Let the nonspecialist in economics pick up a journal article or monograph today and contrast it with one of a generation ago, and the first thing that will strike him is the incomprehensibility of the modern product. The older work was written in ordinary language and, with moderate effort, was comprehensible to the layman; the current work is virtually all mathematics, algebraic or geometric. As one distinguished economist has lamented, "Economics nowadays often seems like a third-rate subbranch of mathematics," and one, he added, that the mathematician himself does not esteem very highly.

Of course, economics shares this accelerated mathematization with virtually every other field of knowledge, including history and literature. But, laboring under the common notion that it is a science with a special focus on *quantities,* economics has proceeded farther and faster than any of its sister disciplines down the mathematical and statistical road.

The emphasis on mathematics is a symptom of a deeper change in the discipline: the rapid adoption of what we may broadly call "positivism" as the guide for research and the criterion for the successful construction of economic theory. The growing influence of positivism has its source in the attempt of all social sciences to mimic the (allegedly) supremely successful science, physics. For social scientists, as for almost all intellectuals, physics has unfortunately all but replaced philosophy as the "queen of the sciences." In the hands of the positivists, philosophy has almost come to seem an elaborate running commentary on and explication of physics, too often serving as the handmaiden of that prestigious science. What positivists see as the methodology of physics has been elevated, at their hands, to be *the* scientific method, and any deviant approach has been barred from the status of science because it does not meet the rigorous positivist test.

At the risk of oversimplification, the positivist model of the scientific method may be summarized as follows:

Step 1. The scientist observes empirical regularities, or "laws," between variables.

Step 2. Hypothetical explanatory generalizations are constructed, from which the empirically observed laws can be deduced and thus "explained."

Step 3. Since competing hypotheses can be framed, each explaining the body of empirical laws, such "coherence" or consistent explanation is not enough; to validate the hypotheses, *other* deductions must be made from them, which must be "testable" by empirical observation.

Step 4. From the construction and testing of hypotheses, a wider and wider body of generalizations is developed; these can be discarded if empirical tests invalidate them, or be replaced by new explanations covering a still wider range of phenomena.

Since the number of variables is virtually infinite, the testing in Step 3, as well as much of the observation in Step 1, can only be done in "controlled experiments," in which all variables but the ones under study are held constant. Replicating the experimental conditions should then replicate the results.

Note that in this methodology we proceed from that which is known with *certainty*—the empirical regularities—up through even wider and more tentative hypotheses. It is this fact that leads the layman to believe erroneously that Newton "overthrew" his predecessors and was in his turn "overthrown" by Einstein. In fact, what happens is not so much substitution as the addition of more general explanations for a wider range of phenomena; the generalizations of a Newton or an Einstein *are* far more tentative than the fact that two molecules of hydrogen combine with one molecule of oxygen to produce water.

Now, I am not expert enough in the philosophy of science to challenge this positivist model of the methodology of physics, although my reading in the philosophy of nature leads me to suspect that it is highly inadequate.[1] My contention is rather that the wholesale and uncritical application of this model to economics in recent decades has led the entire discipline badly astray.

There is, however, unbeknownst to most present-day economists, a competing methodological tradition. This tradition, the method of most of the older classical economists, has been called "praxeology" by Ludwig von Mises, its most eminent modern theorist and practitioner. Praxeology holds that in the social sciences where human beings and human choices are involved, Step 3 is impossible, since even in the most ambitious totalitarian society, it is impossible to hold *all* the variables constant. There *cannot* be controlled experiments when we confront the real world of human activity.

Let us take a recent example of a generally unwelcome economic phenomenon: the accelerated price inflation in the United States in the last few years. There are all manner of competing theoretical explanations for this, ranging from increases in the money supply to a sudden increase in greed on the part of the public or various segments thereof. There is no positivist-empirical way of deciding between these various theories; there is no way of confirming or disproving them by keeping all but one supposedly explanatory variable constant, and then changing that variable to see what happens to prices. In addition, there is the well-known social science analogue of the Heisenberg uncertainty principle: positivist science contains predictions, but how can predictions be tested when the very act of prediction itself changes the forces at work? Thus, economist A predicts a severe recession in six months; acting on this, the government takes measures to

[1] On this, *see* Andrew G. Van Melsen, *The Philosophy of Nature* (Pittsburgh: Duquesne University Press, 1953).

combat the supposedly imminent recession, the public and the stock market react, and so on. The recession then never takes place. Does that mean that the economist was basing his prediction on erroneous theories, or that the theories were correct but inappropriate to the actual data, *or* that he was "really" right but that prompt action forestalled the dreaded event? There is no way to decide.

One further example: Keynesian economists hold that depressions can be cured by massive doses of deficit spending by the government. The United States government engaged in large-scale deficit-spending to combat the depression in the late 1930s, but to no avail. The anti-Keynesians charge that this failure proves the incorrectness of Keynesian theory; the Keynesians reply that the doses were simply not massive enough, and that far greater deficits would have turned the tide. Again, there is no positivist-empirical way to decide between these competing claims.

Praxeologists share the contention of the impossibility of empirical testing with other critics of positivism, such as the institutionalists, who for this reason abandon economic theory altogether and confine themselves to purely empirical or institutional economic reportage. But the praxeologist does not despair; he turns instead to another methodology that *can* yield a correct body of economy theory. This methodology begins with the conviction that while the economist, unlike the physicist, cannot test his hypotheses in controlled experiments, he is, in another sense, in a *better* position than the physicist. For while the physicist is certain of his empirical laws but tentative and uncertain of his explanatory generalizations, the economist is in the opposite position. He begins, not with detailed, quantitative, empirical regularities, but with broad explanatory generalizations. These fundamental premises he knows with certainty; they have the status of apodictic axioms, on which he can build deductively with confidence. Beginning with the certain knowledge of the basic explanatory axiom A, he deduces the implications of A: B, C, and D. From these he deduces further implications, and so on. If he knows that A is true, and if A implies B, C, and D, then he knows with certainty that B, C, and D are true as well. The positivist, looking through the blinders imposed by his notion of physics, finds it impossible to understand how a science can possibly begin with the explanatory axioms and work downward to the more concrete empirical laws. He therefore dismisses the praxeological approach as "mythical" and "apriorist."

What are these axioms with which the economist can so confidently begin? They are the existence, the nature, and the implications of human action. Individual human beings exist. Moreover, they do not simply "move," as do unmotivated atoms or molecules; they *act*, i.e., they have goals and they make choices of means to attain their goals. They order their values or ends in a hierarchy according to whether they attribute greater or lesser importance to them; and they have what they believe is technological knowledge to achieve their goals. All of this action must also take place through time and in a certain space. It is on this basic and evident axiom of human action that the entire structure of praxeological economic theory is built. We do not know, and may never know with certainty, the ultimate equation that will explain all electromagnetic and gravitational phenomena; but we *do* know that people act to achieve goals. And this knowledge is enough to elaborate the body of economic theory.[2]

There is considerable controversy over the empirical status of the praxeological axiom. Professor Mises, working within a Kantian philosophical framework, maintained that like the "laws of thought," the axiom is a priori to human experience and hence apodictically certain. This analysis has given rise to the designation of praxeology as "extreme apriorism." Most praxeologists, however, hold that the axiom is based squarely in empirical reality, which makes it no less certain than it is in Mises's formulation. If the axiom is empirically true, then the logical consequences built upon it must be empirically true as well. But this is not the sort of empiricism welcomed by the positivist, for it is

---

[2]Thus the fact that people must act to achieve their goals implies that there is a scarcity of means to attain them; otherwise the goals would already have been attained. Scarcity implies costs, which in a monetary system (developed much later in the logical elaboration) are reflected in prices, and so forth. For a consciously praxeological development of economic theory, *see* Ludwig von Mises, *Human Action* (New Haven: Yale University Press, 1949), and Murray N. Rothbard, *Man, Economy, and State,* 2d ed. (Kansas City: Sheed Andrews and McMeel, 1970).

based on universal reflective or inner experience, as well as on external physical experience. Thus, the knowledge that human beings have goals and act purposively to attain them rests, not simply on observing that human beings exist, but also on the introspective knowledge of what it means to be human possessed by each man, who then assents to this knowledge. While this sort of empiricism rests on broad knowledge of human action, it is also prior to the complex historical events that economists attempt to explain.

Alfred Schutz pointed out and elaborated the complexity of the interaction between the individual and other persons, the "interpretive understanding" or *Verstehen,* upon which this universal, prescientific knowledge rests. The common-sense knowledge of the universality of motivated, intentional human action, ignored by positivists as "unscientific," actually provides the indispensable groundwork on which science itself must develop.[3] For Schutz this knowledge is empirical, "provided that we do not restrict this term to sensory perceptions of objects and events in the outer world but include the experiential form, by which common-sense thinking in everyday life understands human actions and their outcome in terms of their underlying motives and goals."[4]

The nature of the evidence on which the praxeological axiom rests is, moreover, fundamentally similar to that accepted by the self-proclaimed empiricists. To them, the laboratory experiment is evidence because the sensory experience involved in it is available to each observer; the experience becomes "evident" to all. Logical proof is in this sense similar; for the knowledge that B

---

[3] "It is . . . not understandable that the same authors who are convinced that no verification is possible for the intelligence of other human beings have such confidence in the principle of verifiability itself, which can be realized only through cooperation with others by mutual control." Alfred Schutz, *Collected Papers,* vol. 2, *Studies in Social Theory,* ed. A. Brodersen (The Hague: Nijhoff, 1964), p. 4.

[4] Alfred Schutz, *Collected Papers,* vol. 1, *The Problem of Social Reality,* ed. Maurice Natanson (The Hague: Nijhoff, 1962), p. 65; *see also* pp. 1-66, as well as Peter Winch, "Philosophical Bearings," and Maurice Natanson, "A Study in Philosophy and the Social Sciences," in *Philosophy of the Social Sciences: A Reader,* ed. Maurice Natanson (New York: Random House, 1963). On the importance of the common-sense, prescientific presuppositions of science from a slightly different philosophical perspective, *see* Van Melsen, *Philosophy of Nature,* pp. 6-29.

follows from A becomes evident to all who care to follow the demonstration. In the same way, the fact of human action and of purposive choice also becomes evident to each person who bothers to contemplate it; it is just as evident as the direct sense experience of the laboratory.

From this philosophical perspective, then, all disciplines dealing with human beings — from philosophy to history, psychology, and the social sciences — must take as their starting point the fact that humans engage in motivated, purposive action and are thus different from the unmotivated atoms and stones that are the objects of the physical sciences. But where, then, does praxeology or economics differ from the other disciplines that treat human beings? The difference is that, to the praxeologist, economic *theory* (as distinct from applied economics, which will be treated below) deals, not with the content of human valuations, motivations, and choices, but with the formal fact *that* people engage in such motivated action. Other disciplines focus on the content of these values and actions. Thus, psychology asks how and why people adopt values and make choices; ethics deals with the problem of what values and choices they *should* adopt; technology explains how they should act in order to arrive at chosen ends; and history tries to explain the content of human motives and choices through recorded time. Of these disciplines, history is perhaps the most purely *verstehende,* for the historian is constantly attempting to describe, understand, and explain the motivations and choices of individual actors. Economic theory, on the other hand, is the least *verstehende,* for while it too begins with the axiom of purposive and intentional human action, the remainder of its elaborated structure consists of the deduced logical—and therefore true—implications of that primordial fact.

An example of the formal structure of economic theory is the well-known economic law, built up from the axiom of the existence of motivated human action, that if the demand for any product increases, given the existing supply, the price of that product will rise. This law holds regardless of the ethical or aesthetic status of the product, just as the law of gravity applies to objects regardless of their particular identity. The economic theorist is not interested in the content of what is being demanded, or in its ethical meaning—it may be guns or butter or even textbooks on philosophy. It is this universal, formal nature of economic law that has earned it among laymen the reputation of being cold, heartless, and excessively logical.

Having discussed the nature of the axiom on which the praxeological view of economics is grounded, we may now turn to examine the deductive process itself, the way in which the structure of economic laws is developed, the nature of those laws, and, finally, the ways in which the praxeological economist applies these economic laws to the social world.

One of the basic tools for the deduction of the logical implications of the axiom of human action is the use of the *Gedankenexperiment,* or "mental experiment." The *Gedankenexperiment* is the economic theorist's substitute for the natural scientist's controlled laboratory experiment. Since the relevant variables of the social world cannot actually be held constant, the economist holds them constant in his imagination. Using the tool of verbal logic, he mentally investigates the causal influence of one variable on another. The economist finds, for example, that the price of a product is determined by two variables, the demand for it and its supply at any given time. He then mentally holds the supply constant, and finds that an increase in demand—brought about by higher rankings of the product on the value scales of the public— will bring about an increase in price. Similarly, he finds, again using verbal deductive logic, that if these value scales, and therefore public demand, are mentally held constant, and the supply of the product increases, its price will fall. In short, economics arrives at *ceteris paribus* laws: *Given* the supply, the price will change in the same direction as demand; *given* the demand, price will change in the opposite direction from supply.

One important aspect of these economic laws must be pointed out: They are necessarily *qualitative*. The fact that human beings have goals and preferences, that they make choices to attain their goals, that all action must take place over time, all these are qualitative axioms. And since only the qualitative enters into the logical process from the real world, only the qualitative can emerge. One can only say, for example, that an increase in demand, given the supply, will raise the price; one *cannot* say that a

20 percent increase in demand will bring about a 25 percent increase in price. The praxeologist must reject all attempts, no matter how fashionable, to erect a theory consisting of alleged quantitative laws. In an age that tries desperately to imitate prestigious physics, with its emphasis on mathematics and its quantitative laws, many social scientists, including many economists, have ignored this methodology because of this very insistence on the qualitative bounds of the discipline.

There is a basic reason for the quantity-quality dichotomy between the physical and the social sciences. The objects of physical science do not act; they do not choose, change their minds, and choose again. Their natures may therefore be investigated, and the investigations replicated indefinitely, with quantitative precision. But people do change their minds, and their actions, all the time; their behavior cannot be predicted with exact and therefore scientific precision. Among the many factors helping to determine the demand and the supply of butter, for example, are the valuations placed by each consumer on butter relative to all other products available, the availability of substitutes, the climate in the butter-producing areas, technological methods of producing butter (and margarine), the price of cattle feed, the supply of money in the country, the existence of prosperity or recession in the economy, and the public's expectations of the trend of general prices. Every one of these factors is subject to continuing and unpredictable change. Even if one mammoth equation could be discovered to "explain" all recorded prices of butter for the past 50 years, there is no guarantee, and not even the likelihood, that the equation would have anything to do with *next* month's price.

In fact, if empirical success is the test, it is surely noteworthy that all the determined efforts of quantitative economists, econometricians, and social scientists have not been able to find one single quantitative constant in human affairs. The mathematical laws in the physical sciences contain numerous constants; but the imitative method in the social sciences is proven vain by the fact that not a single constant has ever emerged. Moreover, despite the use of sophisticated econometric models and high-speed computers, the success rate of forecasting economic quantities has been dismal, even for the simplest of aggregates such as the Gross

National Product, let alone for more difficult quantities; the record of GNP forecasting by economists has been poorer than a simple layman's extrapolation of recent trends.[5] In fact, the federal government has had notably poor success even in forecasting the one variable under its own absolute control—its *own* expenditure in the near future. Perhaps we will revise our critical opinion of econometric science if and when the econometricians prove themselves able to make flawless predictions of activity on the stock market—and make themselves vast fortunes in the process.

Except for the fact that they are not quantitative, however, the predictions of the praxeologist are precisely the same kind as those of the natural scientist. The latter, after all, is not a prophet or soothsayer; his successful prediction is not what *will* happen in the world, but what *would* happen if such and such should occur. The scientist can predict successfully that if hydrogen and oxygen are combined in proportions of two to one, the result will be water; but he has no way of predicting scientifically how many scientists in how many laboratories will perform this process at any given period in the future. In the same way, the praxeologist can say, with absolute certainty, that if the demand for butter increases, and the supply remains the same, the price of butter will rise; but he does not know whether the public's demand for butter will in fact rise or fall, let alone by how much it will change. Like the physical scientist, the economist is not a prophet, and it is unfortunate that the econometricians and quantitative economists should have so eagerly assumed this social role.[6]

The English economist John Jewkes suggests the properly limited role for economic forecasting, as well as for applied economics generally:

[5] *See* Victor Zarnowitz, *An Appraisal of Short-Term Economic Forecasts* (New York: National Bureau of Economic Research, 1967). For a record of the problems of forecasting, *see* "Bad Year for Econometrics," *Business Week,* December 20, 1969, pp. 36-40.

[6] The English economist P. T. Bauer properly distinguishes between scientific prediction and forecasting: "Prediction, in the sense of the assessment of the results of specified occurrences or conditions, must be distinguished from the forecasting of future events. Even if the prediction that the producers of a particular crop respond to a higher price by producing more is correct, this prediction does

I submit that economists cannot, without stepping outside their discipline, predict in the sense of telling us what will happen in the future. . . .

In the most general sense, there is, indeed, no such thing as the *economic* future. There is only *the* future in which economic factors are bound together, inextricably and quite without hope of separate identification, with the whole universe of forces determining the course of events. . . . Anyone who proposes to look at it [the future] before the event must take as his province the whole of experience and knowledge. He must cease to behave as a specialist, which means that he must cease to behave as an economist. . . .

The economist's claim to predictive authority must be false in that it leads to a palpable absurdity. If the economic future can, indeed, be described, why not also the scientific future, the political future, the social future, the future in each and every sense? Why should we not be able to plumb all the mysteries of future time?[7]

What, then, is the praxeological view of the function of applied economics? The praxeologist contrasts, on the one hand, the body of qualitative, nomothetic laws developed by economic theory, and on the other, a myriad of unique, complex historical facts of both the past and the future. It is ironic that while the praxeologist is generally denounced by the positivist as an "extreme apriorist," he actually has a far more empirical attitude toward the facts of history. For the positivist is always attempting to compress complex historical facts into artificial molds, regarding them as homogeneous and therefore manipulable and predictable by mechanical, statistical, and quantitative operations in the attempt to find leads, lags, correlations, econometric relations, and "laws of history." This procrustean distortion is undertaken in the belief that the events of human history can be treated in the same mechanistic way as the movements of atoms or molecules— simple, unmotivated, homogeneous elements. The positivist

not enable us to forecast accurately next year's output (still less the harvest in the more distant future), which in the event will be affected by many factors besides changes in price." Peter T. Bauer, *Economic Analysis and Policy in Under-developed Countries* (Durham, N.C.: Duke University Press, 1957), pp. 10-11; *see also* pp. 28-32.

[7] John Jewkes, "The Economist and Economic Change," in *Economics and Public Policy* (Washington, D.C.: Brookings Institution, 1955), pp. 82-83.

thereby ignores the fact that while atoms and stones have no history, man, by virtue of his acts of conscious choice, creates a history. The praxeologist, in contrast, holds that each historical event is the highly complex result of a large number of causal forces, and, further, that it is unique and cannot be considered homogeneous to any other event. Obviously, there are similarities between events, but there is no perfect homogeneity and therefore no room for historical "laws" similar to the exact laws of physical science.

While accepting that there are no mechanical laws of history, however, the praxeologist holds that he can and must use his knowledge of other nomothetic sciences as part of his *verstehende* attempt to understand and explain the idiographic events of history. Let us suppose that the economic historian, or the student of applied economics, is attempting to explain a rapid rise in the price of wheat in a certain country during a certain period. He may bring many nomothetic sciences to bear: The sciences of agronomy and entomology may help reveal that an insect mentioned in the historical record was responsible for a drastic fall in wheat production; meteorological records may show that rainfall was insufficient; he may discover that during the period people's taste for bread increased, perhaps imitating a similar preference by the king; he may discover that the money supply was increasing, and learn from economic theory that an increase in the supply of money tends to raise prices in general, including therefore the price of wheat. And, finally, economic theory states that the price of wheat moves inversely with the supply and directly with the demand. The economic historian combines all of his scientific knowledge with his understanding of motives and choices to attempt to explain the complex historical phenomenon of the price of bread.

A similar procedure is followed in the study of such infinitely more complex historical problems as the causes of the French Revolution, where, again, the historian must blend his knowledge of causal theories in economics, military strategy, psychology, technology, and so on, with his understanding of the motives and choices of individual actors. While historians may well agree on the enumeration of all the relevant causal factors in the problem, they will differ on the weight to be attached to each factor. The evaluation of the relative importance of historical factors is an art, not a science, a matter of personal judgment, experience, and *verstehende* insight which will differ from one historian to another. In this sense, economic historians, like economists (and indeed other historians), can come to qualitative but not quantitative agreement.

For the praxeologist, forecasting is a task very similar to the work of the historian. The latter attempts to "predict" the events of the past by explaining their antecedent causes; similarly, the forecaster attempts to predict the events of the future on the basis of present and past events already known. He uses all his nomothetic knowledge, economic, political, military, psychological, and technological; but at best his work is an art rather than an exact science. Thus, some forecasters will inevitably be better than others, and the superior forecasters will make the more successful entrepreneurs, speculators, generals, and bettors on elections or football games.

The economic forecaster, as Professor Jewkes pointed out, is only looking at part of a tangled and complex social whole. To return to our original example, when he attempts to forecast the price of butter, he must take into consideration the qualitative economic law that price depends directly on demand and inversely on supply; it is then up to him, using knowledge and insight into general economic conditions as well as the specific economic, technological, political, and climatological conditions of the butter market, as well as the values people are likely to place on butter, to try to forecast the movements of the supply and demand of butter, and therefore its price, as accurately as possible. At best, he will have nothing like a perfect score, for he will run aground on the fact of free will altering values and choices, and the consequent impossibility of making exact predictions of the future.[8]

[8] We may mention here the well-known refutation of the notion of predicting the future by Karl Popper, namely, that in order to predict the future, we would have to predict what knowledge we will possess in the future. But we cannot do so, for if we knew what our future knowledge would be, we would *already* be in possession of that knowledge at the present time. See Karl R. Popper, *The Poverty of Historicism* (New York: Harper & Row, 1964), pp. vi-viii.

2. The Praxeological Tradition

The praxeological tradition has a long history in economic thought. We will indicate briefly the outstanding figures in the development of that tradition, especially since these economic methodologists and their views have been recently neglected by economists steeped in the positivist world view.

One of the first self-conscious methodologists in the history of economics was the early 19th century French economist Jean-Baptiste Say. In the lengthy introduction to his magnum opus, *A Treatise on Political Economy,* Say laments that people

> are too apt to suppose that absolute truth is confined to the mathematics and to the results of careful observation and experiment in the physical sciences; imagining that the moral and political sciences contain no invariable facts of indisputable truth, and therefore cannot be considered as genuine sciences, but merely hypothetical systems. . . .

Say could easily have been referring to the positivists of our day, whose methodology prevents them from recognizing that absolute truths can be arrived at in the social sciences, when grounded, as they are in praxeology, on broadly evident axioms. Say insists that the "general facts" underlying what he calls the "moral sciences" are undisputed and grounded on universal observation.

> Hence the advantage enjoyed by every one who, from distinct and accurate observation, can establish the existence of these general facts, demonstrate their connexion, and deduce their consequences. They as certainly proceed from the nature of things as the laws of the material world. We do not imagine them; they are results disclosed to us by judicious observation and analysis. . . . That can be admitted by every reflecting mind.

45

These general facts, according to Say, are "principles," and the science of

> political economy, in the same manner as the exact sciences, is composed of a few fundamental principles, and of a great number of corollaries or conclusions drawn from these principles. It is essential, therefore, for the advancement of this science that these principles should be strictly deduced from observation; the number of conclusions to be drawn from them may afterwards be either multipled or diminished at the discretion of the inquirer, according to the object he proposes.[9]

Here Say has set forth another important point of the praxeological method: that the paths in which the economist works out the implications of the axioms and the elaborated system which results will be decided by his own interests and by the kind of historical facts he is examining. Thus, it is theoretically possible to deduce the theory of money even in an economy of primitive barter, where no money exists; but it is doubtful whether a primitive praxeologist would have bothered to do so.

Interestingly enough, Say at that early date saw the rise of the statistical and mathematical methods, and rebutted them from what can be described as a praxeological point of view. The difference between political economy and statistics is precisely the difference between political economy (or economic theory) and history. The former is based with certainty on universally observed and acknowledged general principles; therefore, "a perfect knowledge of the principles of political economy may be obtained, inasmuch as all the general facts which compose this science may be discovered." Upon these "undeniable general facts," "rigorous deductions" are built, and to that extent political economy "rests upon an immovable foundation." Statistics, on the other hand, only records the ever changing pattern of particular facts, statistics "like history, being a recital of facts, more or less uncertain and necessarily incomplete." Furthermore, Say anticipated the praxeologist's view of historical and statistical data as themselves complex facts needing to be explained. "The study of statistics may gratify curiosity, but it can never be pro-

[9] Jean-Baptiste Say, *A Treatise on Political Economy,* trans. C. C. Biddle (New York: Kelley, 1964), pp. xxiv, xxv, xlv, xxvi.

ductive of advantage when it does not indicate the origin and consequences of the facts it has collected; and by indicating their origin and consequences, it at once becomes the science of political economy." Elsewhere in the essay, Say scoffs at the gullibility of the public toward statistics: "Sometimes, moreover, a display of figures and calculations imposes upon them; as if numerical calculations alone could prove any thing, and as if any rule could be laid down, from which an inference could be drawn without the aid of sound reasoning."[10]

Say goes on to question sharply the value of mathematics in the construction of economic theory, once again referring back to the structure of the basic axioms, or general principles, for his argument. For political economy is concerned with men's values, and these values being "subject to the influence of the faculties, the wants and the desires of mankind, they are not susceptible of any rigorous appreciation, and cannot therefore furnish any data for absolute calculations. In political science, all that is essential is a knowledge of the connexion between causes and their consequences." Delving deeper into the then only embryonic use of the mathematical method in economics, Say points out that the laws of economics are strictly qualitative: "We may, for example, know that for any given year the price of wine will infallibly depend upon the quantity to be sold, compared with the extent of the demand." But "if we are desirous of submitting these two data to mathematical calculation," then it becomes impossible to arrive at precise quantitative forecasts of the innumerable, ever changing forces at work: the climate, the quantity of the harvest, the quality of the product, the stock of wine held over from the previous vintage, the amount of capital, the possibilities of export, the supply of substitute beverages, and the changeable tastes and values of the consumers.[11]

Say offers a highly perceptive insight into the nature and probable consequences of the application of mathematics to economics. He argues that the mathematical method, with its seeming exactitude, can only gravely distort the analysis of qualitative

[10] Ibid., pp. xix-xx, li.
[11] Ibid., pp. xxvi, xxvi n.

human action by stretching and oversimplifying the legitimate insights of economic principles:

> Such persons as have pretended to do it, have not been able to enunciate these questions into analytical language, without divesting them of their natural complication, by means of simplifications, and arbitrary suppressions, of which the consequences, not properly estimated, always essentially change the condition of the problem, and pervert all its results; so that no other inference can be deduced from such calculations than from formula arbitrarily assumed.[12]

In contrast to the physical sciences where the explanatory laws or general principles are always in the realm of the hypothetical, in praxeology it is fatal to introduce oversimplification and falsehood into the premises, for then the conclusions deduced from them will be irredeemably faulty as well.[13]

If mathematics and statistics do not provide the proper method for the political economist, what method is appropriate? The same course that he would pursue in his daily life. "He will examine the immediate elements of the proposed problem, and after having ascertained them with certainty . . . will approximately value their mutual influences with the intuitive quickness of an enlightened understanding. . . ."[14] In short, the laws of the political economist are certain, but their blending and application to any given historical event is accomplished, not by pseudo-quantitative or mathematical methods, which distort and over-

---

[12] Ibid., p. xxvi n.

[13] One of the most pernicious aspects of the current dominance of positivist methodology in economics has been precisely this injection of false premises into economic theory. The leading extreme positivist in economics, Milton Friedman, goes so far as to extol the use of admittedly false premises in the theory, since, according to Friedman, the *only* test of a theory is whether it predicts successfully. *See* Milton Friedman, "The Methodology of Positive Economics," in *Essays in Positive Economics* (Chicago: University of Chicago Press, 1953), pp. 3-46. Of the numerous critiques and discussions of the Friedman thesis, *see* in particular Eugene Rotwein, "On 'The Methodology of Positive Economics,'" *Quarterly Journal of Economics* 73 (November 1959):554-575; Paul A. Samuelson, "Discussion," *American Economic Review, Papers and Proceedings* 53 (May 1963):231-236; Jack Meltz, "Friedman and Machlup on the Significance of Testing Economic Assumptions," *Journal of Political Economy* 73 (February 1965): 37-60.

[14] Say, *Treatise on Political Economy,* p. xxvi n.

simplify, but only by the use of *Verstehen*, "the intuitive quickness of an enlightened understanding."

The first economists to devote their attention specifically to methodology were three leading economists of mid-19th-century Britain: John E. Cairnes, Nassau W. Senior, and John Stuart Mill. Cairnes and Senior, at least, may be considered as proto-praxeologists. Cairnes, after agreeing with Mill that there can be no controlled experiments in the social sciences, adds that the latter have, however, a crucial advantage over the physical sciences. For, in the latter,

> *mankind have no direct knowledge of ultimate physical principles.* The law of gravitation and the laws of motion are among the best established and most certain of such principles; but what is the evidence on which they rest? We do not find them in our consciousness, by reflecting on what passes in our minds; nor can they be made apparent to our sense . . . the proof of all such laws ultimately resolving itself into this, that, assuming them to exist, they account for the phenomena.

In contrast, however,

> *The economist starts with a knowledge of ultimate causes.* He is already, at the outset of his enterprise, in the position which the physicist only attains after ages of laborious research. If any one doubt this, he has only to consider what the ultimate principles governing economic phenomena are . . . : certain mental feelings and certain animal propensities in human beings; [and] the physical conditions under which production takes place. . . . For the discovery of such premises no elaborate process of induction is needed . . . for this reason, that we have, or may have if we choose to turn our attention to the subject, direct knowledge of these causes in our consciousness of what passes in our own minds, and in the information which our senses convey . . . to us of external facts. Every one who embarks in any industrial pursuit is conscious of the motives which actuate him in doing so. He knows that he does so from a desire, for whatever purpose, to possess himself of wealth; he knows that, according to his lights, he will proceed toward his end in the shortest way open to him. . . .[15]

[15] J. E. Cairnes, *The Character and Logical Method of Political Economy* (1857; 2d ed., London: Macmillan, 1875, repr. 1888), pp. 83, 87-88 (italics Cairnes's). The emphasis of Cairnes and other classical economists on wealth as the goal of economic action has been modified by later praxeological economists to include all manner of psychological satisfactions, of which those stemming from material wealth are only a subset. A discussion similar to that of Cairnes can be found in F. A. Hayek, "The Nature and History of the Problem," in Hayek, ed., *Collectivist Economic Planning* (London: Routledge, 1935), pp. 10-11.

Cairnes goes on to point out that the economist uses the mental experiment as a replacement for the laboratory experiment of the physical scientist.

Cairnes demonstrates that deduced economic laws are "tendency," or "if-then," laws, and, moreover, that they are necessarily qualitative, and cannot admit of mathematical or quantitative expression. Thus, he too makes the point that it is impossible to determine precisely how much the price of wheat will rise in response to a drop in supply; for one thing, "it is evident that the disposition of people to sacrifice one kind of gratification to another—to sacrifice vanity to comfort, or decency to hunger—is not susceptible of precise measurement. . . ."[16] In the preface to his second edition, two decades later in 1875, Cairnes reiterated his opposition to the growing application of the mathematical method to economics, which, in contrast to its use in the physical sciences, cannot produce new truths; "and unless it can be shown either that mental feelings admit of being expressed in precise quantitative forms, or, on the other hand, that economic phenomena do not depend upon mental feelings, I am unable to see how this conclusion can be avoided."[17]

Cairnes's older contemporary, Nassau Senior, was the most important praxeologist of that era. Before Senior, classical economists such as John Stuart Mill had placed the fundamental premises of economics on the shaky ground of being *hypotheses;* the major hypothesis was that all men act to obtain the maximum of material wealth. Since this is clearly not always true, Mill had to concede that economics was only a hypothetical and approximate science. Senior broadened the fundamental premise to include immaterial wealth or satisfaction, a complete, apodictic, and universally true principle based on insight into the goal-seeking nature of human action.

> In stating that every man desires to obtain additional wealth with as little sacrifice as possible, we must not be supposed to mean that everybody . . . wishes for an indefinite quantity of everything. . . . What we mean to state is that no person feels his whole wants to be adequately supplied; that every person has some unsatisfied desires which he believes that additional wealth would gratify.

[16] Cairnes, *Character and Logical Method,* p. 127.
[17] Ibid., p. v.

50

> The nature and urgency of each individual's wants are as various as the differences in individual character.[18]

In contrast to the physical sciences, Senior pointed out, economics and the other "mental sciences" draw their premises from the universal facts of human consciousness:

> The physical sciences, being only secondarily conversant with mind, draw their premises almost exclusively from observation or hypothesis. Those which treat only of magnitude or number, . . . the pure sciences, draw them altogether from hypothesis. . . . They disregard almost entirely the phenomenon of consciousness. . . .
>
> On the other hand, the mental sciences and the mental arts draw their premises principally from consciousness. The subjects with which they are chiefly conversant are the workings of the human mind.[19]

These latter premises are "a very few general propositions, which are the result of observation, or consciousness, and which almost every man, as soon as he hears them, admits, as familiar to his thought, or at least, as included in his previous knowledge."[20]

During the 1870s and 1880s, classical economics was supplanted by the neoclassical school. In this period the praxeological method was carried on and further developed by the Austrian School, founded by Carl Menger of the University of Vienna and continued by his two most eminent disciples, Eugen von Böhm-Bawerk and Friedrich von Wieser. It was on the basis of their work that Böhm-Bawerk's student Ludwig von Mises later founded praxeology as a self-conscious and articulated methodology.[21] As it was outside the increasingly popular intel-

---

[18] Nassau William Senior, *An Outline of the Science of Political Economy* (1836; repr., New York: Kelley, n.d.), p. 27.

[19] Marian Bowley, *Nassau Senior and Classical Economics* (New York: Kelley, 1949), p. 56.

[20] Ibid., p. 43. *See also* p. 64, where Bowley points out the similarity between Senior's methodological views and the praxeology of Ludwig von Mises.

[21] The outstanding example is Mises, *Human Action. See also* his *Theory and History* (New Haven: Yale University Press, 1957); *The Ultimate Foundation of Economic Science* (Kansas City: Sheed Andrews and McMeel, 1978); and *Epistemological Problems of Economics* (Princeton, N.J.: Van Nostrand, 1960). *See also* F. A. Hayek, *The Counter-Revolution of Science* (Glencoe, Ill.: Free Press, 1955); Lionel Robbins, *An Essay on the Nature and Significance of Economic Science*, 2d ed. (London: Macmillan, 1949); and Israel M. Kirzner, *The Economic Point of View*, 2d ed. (Kansas City: Sheed Andrews and McMeel, 1976).

51

lectual fashion of positivism and mathematics, however, the Austrian School has been greatly neglected in recent years and dismissed as an unsound approximation of the positivist-mathematical theory of the Lausanne School, founded by Léon Walras of Lausanne and continued by the Italian economist and sociologist Vilfredo Pareto.

A few followers or sympathetic observers, however, have carried on investigations into the methodology of the early Austrian School. Leland B. Yeager notes what we now see as the typically praxeological view of the unique advantage of economic theory over the physical sciences: "While the basic elements of theoretical interpretation in the natural sciences, such, he [Menger] says, as forces and atoms, cannot be observed directly, the elements of explanation in economics—human individuals and their strivings —are of a direct empirical nature." Furthermore, "The facts that economists induce from the behavior of themselves and other people serve as axioms from which a useful body of economic theory can be logically deduced, much as in geometry an impressive body of theorems can be deduced from a few axioms." In short, "Menger conceived of economic theory as a body of deductions from basic principles having a strong empirical foundation." Referring to the dominant positivist economists of our own day, Yeager adds perceptively,

> Not sharing . . . Menger's understanding of how empirical content gets into so-called "armchair theory," many economists of our own day apparently regard theoretical and empirical work as two distinct fields. Manipulation of arbitrarily-assumed functional relationships is justified in the minds of such economists by the idea that empirical testing of theories against the real world comes afterward.[22]

Other writers have discovered links between the Austrian method and various strands of the *philosophia perennis.* Thus, Emil Kauder finds a close relationship between this method and Aristotelian philosophy, which was still influential in Austria at the end of the nineteenth century. Kauder points out that all the Austrians were "social ontologists," and that as such they be-

[22] Leland B. Yeager, "The Methodology of Henry George and Carl Menger," *American Journal of Economics and Sociology* 13 (April 1954): 235, 238.

lieved in a structure of reality "both as a logical starting point and as a criterion of validity." He notes Mises's statement that economic laws are "ontological facts," and he characterizes as both ontological and Aristotelian the concern of Menger and his followers to uncover the "essences" of phenomena, rather than to treat superficial and complex economic quantities. Kauder also points out that for Menger and the Austrians, economic theory deals with types and typical relations, which provide knowledge that transcends the immediate, concrete case and is valid for all times and places. Concrete historical cases are thus the Aristotelian "matter" which contains potentialities, while the laws and types are the Aristotelian "forms" which actualize the potential. For the Austrians, and especially for Böhm-Bawerk, furthermore, causality and teleology were identical. In contrast to the functional-mutual determination approach of Walras and of contemporary economists, the Austrians traced the causes of economic phenomena back to the wants and choices of consumers. Wieser especially stressed the grounding of economic theory on the inner experience of the mind.[23]

Furthermore, Ludwig M. Lachmann, in contrasting the Austrian and Lausanne Schools, shows that the Austrians were endeavoring to construct a "*verstehende* social science," the same ideal that Max Weber was later to uphold. Lachmann points out that the older Ricardian economists adopted the "objective" method of the natural sciences insofar as their major focus was upon the quantitative problem of income distribution. In their analysis, factors of production (land, labor, and capital goods) react mechanically to external economic changes. But, in contrast, "Austrian Theory is 'subjective' also in the sense that individuals . . . perform acts and lend the imprint of their individuality to the events on the market." As for the contrast between Austria and Lausanne,

> it is the contrast between those [Lausanne] who confine themselves to determining the appropriate magnitudes of the elements of a system (the conditions of equilibrium) and those [the Aus-

[23] Emil Kauder, "Intellectual and Political Roots of the Older Austrian School," *Zeitschrift für Nationalökonomie* 17, no. 4 (1958):411-425.

> trians] who try to explain events in terms of the mental acts of the individuals who fashion them. Most Austrian thinkers were dimly aware of this contrast, but before Hans Mayer, Mises and Hayek were unable to express it concisely. The validity of the Lausanne model is limited to a stationary world. The background of the Austrian theory, by contrast, is a world of continuous change in which plans have to be conceived and continually revised.[24]

We may conclude this sketch of the history of the praxeological tradition in economics by treating an important but much neglected debate on economic methodology which occurred at the turn of the 20th century between Pareto and the philosopher Benedetto Croce. Croce, from his own highly developed praxeological position, opened the debate by chiding Pareto for having written that economic theory was a species of mechanics. Vigorously rejecting this view, Croce points out that a fact in mechanics is a mere fact, which requires no positive or negative comment; whereas words of approval or disapproval can appropriately be applied to an *economic* fact. The reason is that the true data of economics are not "physical things and objects, but actions. The physical object is merely the brute matter of an economic act. . . ."[25] Economic data, then, are acts of man, and these acts are

---

[24] English abstract of Ludwig M. Lachmann, "Die geistesgeschichtliche Bedeutung der österreichischen Schule in der Volkwirtschaftslehre," *Zeitschrift für National-ökonomie* 26, nos. 1-3 (1966): 152-167, in *Journal of Economic Abstracts* 5 (September 1967):553-554. *See also* Lachmann, "Methodological Individualism and the Market Economy," in *Roads to Freedom: Essays in Honor of Friedrich A. von Hayek,* ed. E. Streissler (New York: Kelley, 1969), pp. 89-103; and Israel M. Kirzner, "Methodological Individualism, Market Equilibrium, and Market Process," *Il Politico* 32, no. 4 (December 1967):787-799.

[25] Benedetto Croce, "On the Economic Principle: I" (1900), *International Economic Papers,* no. 3 (1953), pp. 173, 175. On Croce's views on economics, *see* Giorgio Tagliacozzo, "Croce and the Nature of Economic Science," *Quarterly Journal of Economics* 59 (May 1945):307-329. On the Croce-Pareto debate, *see* Kirzner, *Economic Point of View,* pp. 155-157.

It is of interest that the Walrasian economist Joseph Schumpeter, in his only untranslated work, *Das Wesen und der Hauptinhalt der theoretischen National-ökonomie* (Leipzig: Duncker and Humblot, 1908), specifically declared that the economist must only treat changes in "economic quantities" as if they were caused automatically, without reference to the human beings who may have been involved in such changes. In that way, causality and purpose would be replaced in economic theory by functional, mathematical relationships. *See* Kirzner, *Economic Point of View,* pp. 68-70.

the results of conscious choice.

In his lengthy reply, Pareto reiterates the similarity between economics and mechanics, and, like the positivists of today, defends unrealistic mechanistic assumptions as simple abstractions from reality, in the supposed manner of the natural sciences. Professing, in a typical positivist gambit, not to "understand" the concept of value, Pareto writes: "I see . . . that you employ the term *value*. . . . I no longer use it as I do not know what it would convey to other people. . . ." The concept of value is vague and complex and not subject to measurement; therefore, "the equations of pure economics establish relations between quantities of things, hence objective relations, and not relations between more or less precise concepts of our minds."[26] Criticizing Croce's evident concentration on the essences of economic action, as exemplified in his insistence that "one ought to study not the things which are the result of actions but the actions themselves," Pareto complains that this method is an ancient scientific fallacy. "The ancients conjured up cosmogonies instead of studying astronomy, wondered about the principles of the elements water and fire . . . , instead of studying chemistry. Ancient science wanted to proceed from the origin to the facts. Modern science starts from the facts and proceeds towards the origin at an extremely slow pace." Typically, Pareto sets forth the objectivist, positivist position by arguing from the analogy of the method of the natural sciences, thus completely begging the question of whether the methodologies of the natural and the social sciences should or should not be similar. Thus he concludes that "science proceeds by replacing the relationships between human concepts (which relationships are the first to occur to us) by relationships between things."[27]

Croce replies by criticizing Pareto's restriction of economics to measurable quantities as arbitrary; for what of those economic situations where the objects of action or exchange are not measurable? Croce suggests that it is Pareto who is really being meta-

---

[26] Vilfredo Pareto, "On the Economic Phenomenon" (1900), *International Economic Papers,* no. 3, p. 187.

[27] Ibid., pp. 190, 196.

physical, while Croce is the true empiricist. For "your implied metaphysical postulate is . . . this: that the facts of man's activity are of the same nature as physical facts; that in the one case as in the other we can only observe regularity and deduce consequences therefrom, without ever penetrating into the inner nature of the facts. . . . How would you defend this postulate of yours except by a metaphysical monism . . . ?" In contrast, writes Croce, "I hold to experience. This testifies to me of the fundamental distinction between external and internal, between physical and mental, between mechanics and teleology, between passivity and activity. . . ." As for value, it is really a simple term wrapped up in human activity: "Value is observed immediately in ourselves, in our consciousness."[28]

In his rejoinder, Pareto begins with a typical example of metaphysical obtuseness: He does *not* believe that "the facts of man's activity are of the same nature as physical facts" because he doesn't know what "nature" may be. He goes on to reiterate various examples from physical science to demonstrate the proper methodology for all disciplines. He wishes to follow the "masters of positive science" rather than mere philosophers. Pareto concludes with a concise summation of the differences between the two men and the two methodologies:

> We experimentalists . . . accept hypotheses not for any intrinsic value they may have but only in so far as they yield deductions which are in harmony with the facts. You, considering the nature of things independently from the rest, establish a certain proposition A, and from it come down to the concrete facts B. We may accept proposition A, but only as a hypothesis, therefore making not the slightest attempt to prove it. . . . Then we see what can be deduced from it. If those deductions agree with the facts we accept the hypothesis, for the time being of course, because we hold nothing as final or absolute.[29]

[28] Croce, "On the Economic Principle: II" (1901), *International Economic Papers*, no. 3, pp. 198-199.

[29] Pareto, "On the Economic Principle" (1901), *International Economic Papers*, no. 3, p. 206.

3. Methodological Individualism

Only an individual has a mind; only an individual can feel, see, sense, and perceive; only an individual can adopt values or make choices; only an individual can *act*. This primordial principle of "methodological individualism," central to Max Weber's social thought, must underlie praxeology as well as the other sciences of human action. It implies that such collective concepts as groups, nations, and states do not actually exist or act; they are only metaphorical constructs for describing the similar or concerted actions of individuals. There are, in short, no "governments" as such; there are only individuals acting in concert in a "governmental" manner. Max Weber puts it clearly:

> These collectivists must be treated as solely the resultants and modes of organization of the particular acts of individual persons, since these alone can be treated as agents in a course of subjectively understandable action. . . . For sociological purposes . . . there is no such thing as a collective personality which "acts." When reference is made in a sociological context to . . . collectivities, what is meant is . . . *only* a certain kind of development of actual or possible social actions of the individual persons.[30]

Ludwig von Mises points out that what differentiates purely individual action from that of individuals acting as members of a collective is the different *meaning* attached by the people involved.

---

[30] Max Weber, *The Theory of Social and Economic Organization* (Glencoe, Ill.: Free Press, 1957), quoted in Alfred Schutz, *The Phenomenology of the Social World* (Evanston, Ill.: Northwestern University Press, 1967), p. 199. For an application of methodological individualism to foreign policy, *see* Parker T. Moon, *Imperialism and World Politics* (New York: Macmillan, 1930), p. 58. For a more general political application, *see* Frank Chodorov, "Society Are People," in *The Rise and Fall of Society* (New York: Devin-Adair, 1959), pp. 29-37.

> It is the meaning which the acting individuals and all those who are touched by their action attribute to an action, that determines its character. It is the meaning that marks one action as the action of the state or of the municipality. The hangman, not the state, executes a criminal. It is the meaning of those concerned that discerns in the hangman's action an action of the state. A group of armed men occupies a place. It is the meaning of those concerned which imputes this occupation not to the officers and soldiers on the spot, but to their nation.[31]

In his important methodological work, Mises's disciple F. A. Hayek has demonstrated that the fallacy of treating collective constructs as directly perceived "social wholes" ("capitalism," "the nation," "the class") about which laws can be discovered stems from the objectivist-behaviorist insistence on treating men from the outside, as if they were stones, rather than attempting to understand their subjectively determined actions.

> It [the objectivist view] treats social phenomena not as something of which the human mind is a part and the principles of whose organization we can construct from the familiar parts, but as if they were objects directly perceived by us as wholes. . . .
> There is the rather vague idea that since "social phenomena" are to be the object of study, the obvious procedure is to start from the direct observation of these "social phenomena," where the existence in popular usage of such terms as "society" or "economy" is naively taken as evidence that there must be definite "objects" corresponding to them.[32]

Hayek adds that emphasis on the meaning of the individual act brings out that what of social complexes is directly known to us are only the parts and that the whole is never directly perceived but always reconstructed by an effort of our imagination."[33]

Alfred Schutz, the outstanding developer of the phenomenological method in the social sciences, has reminded us of the importance of going back "to the 'forgotten man' of the social sciences, to the actor in the social world whose doing and feeling lies at the bottom of the whole system. We, then, try to understand him in that doing and feeling and the state of mind which

---

[31] Mises, *Human Action*, p. 42.

[32] Hayek, *Counter-Revolution of Science*, pp. 53-54.

[33] Ibid., p. 214.

induced him to adopt specific attitudes towards his social environment." Schutz adds that "for a theory of action the subjective point of view must be retained in its fullest strength, in default of which such a theory loses its basic foundations, namely its reference to the social world of everyday life and experience." Lacking such a foundation, social science is likely to replace the "world of social reality" by a fictional nonexisting world constructed by the scientific observer. Or, as Schutz puts it succinctly: "I cannot understand a social thing without reducing it to human activity which has created it, and beyond it, without referring this human activity to the motives out of which it springs."[34]

Arnold W. Green has recently demonstrated how the use of invalid collective concepts has damaged the discipline of sociology. He notes the increasing use of "society" as an entity which thinks, feels, and acts, and, in recent years, has functioned as the perpetrator of all social ills. "Society," for example, and not the criminal, is often held to be responsible for all crime. In many quarters "society" is considered almost demonic, a "reified villain" which "may be attacked at will, blamed at random, derided and mocked with self-righteous fury, [and] may even be overturned by fiat or utopian yearning—and somehow, in some way, buses will still run on time." Green adds that "if on the other hand, society is viewed as people whose insecure social relationships are preserved only by the fealty paid their common store of moral rules, then the area of free choice available in which with impunity to demand, undermine, and wreck, is sharply restricted." Moreover, if we realize that "society" does not itself exist, but is made up only of individual people, then to say that "society is responsible for crime, and criminals are not responsible for crime, is to say that only those members of society who do not commit crime can be held responsible for crime. Nonsense this obvious can be circumvented only by conjuring up society as devil, as evil being apart from people and what they do."[35]

---

[34] Schutz, *Collected Papers* 2:7, 8, 10.

[35] Arnold W. Green, "The Reified Villain," *Social Research* 35 (Winter 1968):656, 664. On the concept of "society," *see also* Mises, *Theory and History,* pp. 250 ff.

Economics has been rife with fallacies that arise when collective social metaphors are treated as if they were existent objects. Thus, during the era of the gold standard there was occasionally great alarm that "England" or "France" was in mortal danger because "it" was losing gold. What actually happened was that English*men* and French*men* were voluntarily shipping gold overseas and thus threatening the people who ran the banks of those countries with the necessity of meeting obligations to pay in gold which they could not possibly fulfill. But the use of the collective metaphor converted a grave problem of banking into a vague national crisis for which every citizen was somehow responsible.

Similarly, during the 1930s and 1940s many economists proclaimed that in contrast to debts owed overseas, the size of the domestic public debt was unimportant because "we only owe it to ourselves." The implication was that the collective national person owed "himself" money from one pocket to another. This explanation obscured the fact that it makes a substantial difference for every person whether he is a member of the "we" or the "ourselves."

Sometimes the collective concept is treated unabashedly as a biological organism. Thus, the popular concept of economic growth implies that every economy is somehow destined, in the manner of a living organism, to "grow" in some predetermined manner. The use of such analogical terms is an attempt to overlook or even negate individual will and consciousness in social and economic affairs. As Edith Penrose has written in a critique of the use of the "growth" concept in the study of business firms:

> Where explicit biological analogies crop up in economics they are drawn exclusively from that aspect of biology which deals with the unmotivated behavior of organisms. . . . We have no reason whatever for thinking that the growth pattern of a biological organism is *willed* by the organism itself. On the other hand, we have every reason for thinking that the growth of a firm is willed by those who make the decisions of the firm . . . and the proof of this lies in the fact that no one can describe the development of any given firm . . . except in terms of decisions taken by individual men.[36]

[36] Edith Tilton Penrose, "Biological Analogies in the Theory of the Firm," *American Economic Review,* December 1952, p. 808.

There is no better summary of the nature of praxeology and the role of economic theory in relation to concrete historical events than in Alfred Schutz's discussion of the economic methodology of Ludwig von Mises:

> No economic act is conceivable without some reference to an economic actor, but the latter is absolutely anonymous; it is not you, nor I, nor an entrepreneur, nor even an "economic man" as such, but a pure universal "one." This is the reason why the propositions of theoretical economics have just that "universal validity" which gives them the ideality of the "and so forth" and "I can do it again." However, one can study the economic actor as such and try to find out what is going on in his mind; of course, one is not then engaged in theoretical economics but in economic history or economic sociology. . . . However, the statements of these sciences can claim no universal validity, for they deal either with the economic sentiments of particular historical individuals or with types of economic activity for which the economic acts in question are evidence. . . .
>
> In our view, pure economics is a perfect example of an objective meaning-complex about subjective meaning-complexes, in other words, of an objective meaning-configuration stipulating the typical and invariant subjective experiences of anyone who acts within an economic framework. . . . Excluded from such a scheme would have to be any consideration of the uses to which the "goods" are to be put after they are acquired. But once we do turn our attention to the subjective meaning of a real individual person, leaving the anonymous "anyone" behind, then of course it makes sense to speak of behavior that is atypical. . . . To be sure, such behavior is irrelevant from the point of view of economics, and it is in this sense that economic principles are, in Mises' words, "not a statement of what usually happens, but of what necessarily must happen."[37]

---

[37] Schutz, *Phenomenology of the Social World*, pp. 137, 245.

RECOMMENDED READING

Agassi, Joseph. "Methodological Individualism." In *Modes of Individualism and Collectivism,* edited by John O'Neill. New York: St. Martin's Press, 1973.

Blanshard, Brand, *Reason and Analysis.* La Salle, Ill.: Open Court, 1962.

Block, Walter. "A Comment on 'The Extraordinary Claim of Praxeology' by Professor Gutierrez." *Theory and Decision* 3 (1973): 381-382.

Collingwood, R. G. "Economics as a Philosophical Science." *Ethics* 36 (1926):162-185.

Egger, John B. "The Austrian Method." In *New Directions in Austrian Economics,* edited by Louis M. Spadaro. Kansas City: Sheed Andrews and McMeel, 1978.

Hayek, Friedrich A. *The Counter-Revolution of Science: Studies on the Abuse of Reason,* pp. 25-43. Glencoe, Ill.: The Free Press, 1955.

———. *Individualism and Economic Order,* pp. 33-91. Chicago: University of Chicago Press, 1948.

———. *New Studies in Philosophy, Politics, Economics, and the History of Ideas,* pp. 23-34. Chicago: University of Chicago Press, 1978.

———. "The Pretense of Knowledge." In his *Unemployment and Monetary Policy: Government as Generator of the "Business Cycle."* San Francisco: Cato Institute, 1979.

———. *Studies in Philosophy, Politics, and Economics.* Chicago: University of Chicago Press, 1967.

Hicks, J. R., and Weber, Wilhelm, eds. *Carl Menger and the Austrian School of Economics.* Oxford: Clarendon Press, 1973.

Ischboldin, Boris. "A Critique of Econometrics." *Review of Social Economy* 18 (September 1960).

Kauder, Emil. *A History of Marginal Utility Theory.* Princeton, N.J.: Princeton University Press, 1965.

Kirzner, Israel M. *The Economic Point of View: An Essay in the History of Economics.* 2d ed., pp. 146-185. Kansas City: Sheed Andrews and McMeel, 1976.

———. "Methodological Individualism, Market Equilibrium, and Market Process." *Il Politico* 32 (December 1967):787-799.

———. "On the Method of Austrian Economics." In *The Foundations of Modern Austrian Economics,* edited by Edwin G. Dolan, pp. 40-51. Kansas City: Sheed Andrews and McMeel, 1976.

Knight, Frank H. " 'What Is Truth' in Economics." In *On the History and Method of Economics,* edited by William L. Letwin and Alexander J. Morin, pp. 151-178. Chicago: University of Chicago Press, 1956.

Lachmann, Ludwig M. *The Legacy of Max Weber.* Berkeley, Calif.: Glendessary Press, 1971.

———. *Macroeconomic Thinking and the Market Economy.* Menlo Park, Calif.: Institute for Humane Studies, 1978.

———. "The Role of Expectations in Economics as a Social Science," "The Science of Human Action," "Methodological Individualism and the Market Economy," and "Economics as a Social Science." In his *Capital, Expectations, and the Market Process: Essays on the Theory of the Market Economy,* edited by Walter E. Grinder, pp. 65-80, 94-111, 149-165, 166-180. Kansas City: Sheed Andrews and McMeel, 1977.

Leoni, Bruno, and Frola, Eugenio. "On Mathematical Thinking in Economics." *Journal of Libertarian Studies* 1:101-109.

Lukes, Steven. *Individualism,* pp. 110-122. Oxford: Basil Blackwell, 1973.

Menger, Carl. *Principles of Economics.* Glencoe, Ill.: The Free Press, 1950.

———. *Problems in Economics and Sociology.* Edited by L. Schneider. Urbana: University of Illinois Press, 1963.

Mises, Ludwig von. *Epistemological Problems of Economics.* Princeton, N.J.: Van Nostrand, 1960.

———. *Human Action: A Treatise on Economics,* pp. 30-71, 92-102. New Haven: Yale University Press, 1949.

———. "Social Science and Natural Science." *Journal of Social Philosophy and Jurisprudence* 7 (1942):240-253.

————. *Theory and History: An Interpretation of Social and Economic Evolution.* New Haven: Yale University Press, 1957.

————. *The Ultimate Foundation of Economic Science: An Essay on Method.* Kansas City: Sheed Andrews and McMeel, 1978.

Paul, Jeffrey E. "Individualism, Holism and Human Action: An Investigation into Social Scientific Methodology." Ph.D. dissertation, Harvard University, 1974.

Poirier, René. "Logique," In *Vocabulaire Technique et Critique de la Philosophie,* edited by André Lalande, 6th rev. ed., pp. 574-575. Paris: Presses Universitaires de France, 1951.

Popper, Karl R. *The Poverty of Historicism.* New York: Harper & Row, 1964.

Rickert, Heinrich. *Science and History.* Princeton, N.J.: Van Nostrand, 1962.

Rizzo, Mario J. "Praxeology and Econometrics: A Critique of Positivist Economics." In *New Directions in Austrian Economics,* edited by Louis M. Spadaro, pp. 40-56. Kansas City: Sheed Andrews and McMeel, 1978.

Rothbard, Murray N. "In Defense of 'Extreme Apriorism.'" *Southern Economic Journal* 23 (1957):314-320.

————. *Man, Economy, and State: A Treatise on Economic Principles.* 2d ed., pp. 1-66. Kansas City: Sheed Andrews and McMeel, 1970.

————. "Praxeology: The Methodology of Austrian Economics." In *The Foundations of Modern Austrian Economics,* edited by Edwin G. Dolan, pp. 40-51. Kansas City: Sheed Andrews and McMeel, 1976.

————. "Praxeology: Reply to Mr. Schuller." *American Economic Review,* December 1951, pp. 943-946.

————. *Toward a Reconstruction of Utility and Welfare Economics.* New York: Center for Libertarian Studies, 1976.

Schoeck, H., and Wiggins, J. W., eds. *Relativism and the Study of Man.* Princeton, N.J.: Van Nostrand, 1961.

Schutz, Alfred. *The Phenomenology of the Social World.* Evanston, Ill.: Northwestern University Press, 1967.

Sherwood, Sidney. "The Philosophical Basis of Economics." *Annals of the American Academy of Social and Political Science* (1894):58-92.

Stonier, A., and Bode, K. "A New Approach to the Methodology of the Social Sciences." *Economica* (1937):406-424.

Strawson, Philip F. *Individuals: An Essay in Descriptive Metaphysics.* New York: Doubleday, 1963.

Toohey, John L. *Notes on Epistemology.* Washington, D.C.: Georgetown University Press, 1952.

Van Melsen, Andrew G. *The Philosophy of Nature.* Pittsburgh: Duquesne University Press, 1953.

Watkins, J. W. N. "Types of Historical Explanation," "Ideal Historical Explanation in the Social Sciences," "Methodological Individualism: A Reply." In *Modes of Individualism and Collectivism,* edited by John O'Neill. New York: St. Martin's Press, 1973.

White, Lawrence H. *Methodology of the Austrian School.* New York: Center for Libertarian Studies, 1977.

Wild, John, ed. *The Return to Reason: Essays in Realistic Philosophy.* Chicago: Henry Regnery, 1953.

Wild, John, and Cobitz, J. L. "On the Distinction Between the Analytic and Synthetic." *Philosophy and Phenomenological Research* 8 (June 1948):651-667.

Wong, Hao, "Notes on the Analytic-Synthetic Distinction." *Theoria* 21 (1955):158.

ABOUT THE AUTHOR

Murray N. Rothbard received his A.B. in 1945, his A.M. in 1946, and his Ph.D. in economics in 1956—all from Columbia University. He is Professor of Economics at Polytechnic Institute of New York and a Senior Fellow, Cato Institute.

He was an Instructor at City College of New York from 1948 to 1949, a Senior Analyst for the William Volker Fund from 1961 to 1962, and has been an Associate of the University Seminar in the History of Legal and Political Thought at Columbia University since 1964. He is Editor of *The Journal of Libertarian Studies* and Contributing Editor to *Inquiry* magazine and *Libertarian Review*.

Rothbard is the author of *America's Great Depression; The Case for a 100% Gold Dollar; Conceived in Liberty* (3 vols.); *Education: Free and Compulsory; Egalitarianism as a Revolt Against Nature and Other Essays; For a New Liberty: The Libertarian Manifesto; Man, Economy, and State: A Treatise on Economic Principles; The Panic of 1819: Reaction and Policies; Power and Market: Government and the Economy; Toward a Reconstruction of Utility and Welfare Economics; What Has Government Done to Our Money?;* and other works. He is the editor of *Capital, Interest, and Rent: Essays in the Theory of Distribution,* by Frank A. Fetter; and *A New History of Leviathan: Essays on the Rise of the American Corporate State* (with Ronald Radosh). He has contributed to more than 25 books and has written more than 40 articles and reviews for scholarly journals.

The Cato Papers

Reprinted by the Cato Institute, the Papers in this series have been selected for their singular contributions to such fields as economics, history, philosophy, and public policy.

Copies of the *Cato Papers* may be ordered from the Publications Department, Cato Institute, 747 Front Street, San Francisco, California 94111.